MESA VERDE
National Park

THE FIRST 100 YEARS

THE FIRST 100 YEARS

Edited by Rose Houk and Faith Marcovecchio
Duane A. Smith, Historical Consultant

Foreword by Ben Nighthorse Campbell

 MESA VERDE MUSEUM ASSOCIATION AND FULCRUM PUBLISHING

Library of Congress Cataloging-in-Publication Data
Mesa Verde National Park : the first 100 years / edited by Rose Houk and Faith Marcovecchio;
Duane Smith, historical consultant; foreword by Ben Nighthorse Campbell.
    p. cm.
ISBN 1-55591-549-3 (hardcover)—
ISBN 1-55591-552-3 (pbk.)
1. Mesa Verde National Park (Colo.)
History. I. Houk, Rose, 1950- II. Marcovecchio, Faith. III. Smith, Duane A.
    F782.M52M475 2005
    978.8'27--dc22
                                    2005001604
ISBN-13 (hardcover) 978-1-55591-549-0   (pbk.) 978-1-55591-552-0
Printed in China

0 9 8 7 6 5 4 3 2 1

Editorial: Rose Houk, Faith Marcovecchio
Historical Consultant: Duane A. Smith
Design: Christina Watkins and Amanda Summers
Original Essays: Florence Lister, Duane A. Smith, and Ann Haymond Zwinger
Additional Contributions: George San Miguel, Duane A. Smith
Project Manager: Tracey L. Chavis
NPS Liaison: Tessy Shirakawa

Special thanks to Estella Cole, Larry Nordby, Julie Bell, Will Morris, Peter Pino, Kathy McKay, Liz Bauer, Carolyn Landes, Krista Boardman, Flint Boardman, Donna Lee Budd-Jack, Shirley Jones, Kent Thomas, Patti Bell, Robert Jenson, Linda Towle, Marlan Chavis, Kay Barnett, Betty Upchurch, Marc Solomon, Linda Martin, Mesa Verde Board of Directors

This tribute to Mesa Verde National Park would not have been possible without the generous support of the Colorado Historical Society and the State Historical Fund.

Mesa Verde Museum Association
P.O. Box 38
Mesa Verde National Park, CO 81330
(970) 529-4445
www.mesaverde.org

Fulcrum Publishing
16100 Table Mountain Parkway, Suite 300
Golden, CO 80403
(800) 992-2908 • (303) 277-1623
www. fulcrum-books.com

Dedicated to the twenty-four tribes associated with Mesa Verde National Park

Hopi Tribe

Pueblo of Acoma

Pueblo of Cochiti

Pueblo of Isleta

Pueblo of Laguna

Pueblo of Jemez

Pueblo of Nambe

Pueblo of Sandia

Pueblo of San Felipe

The Navajo Nation

Picuris Pueblo

Pueblo of Pojoaque

Pueblo of San Ildefonso

Pueblo of San Juan

Pueblo of Santo Domingo

Santa Clara Pueblo

Santa Ana Pueblo

Southern Ute Tribe

Taos Pueblo

Ute Mountain Ute Tribe

Pueblo of Zia

Ysleta del Sur Pueblo

Pueblo of Zuni

Tesuque Pueblo

CONTENTS

CLOCKWISE: *Mesa Verde kiva pot;* Denver Daily News *clipping; early stabilization crew in Balcony House forging their own steel*

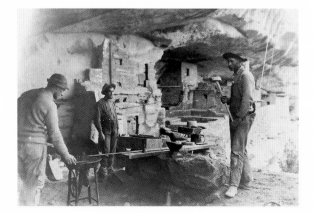

ABOVE: *Painting by Larry Eifert*

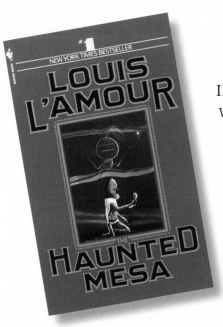

FOREWORD

Two centuries before Columbus arrived in the New World, a people who have come to be known as the Ancestral Puebloans mysteriously left their stone cities to be "discovered" by future generations.

Early Mesa Verdeans raised their children, cultivated their crops, and prayed to their creator, carrying out a way of life that had as its primary tenet that they were part of nature, not the architect of nature. The lessons they left could offer lessons today to educators, doctors, astronomers, farmers, and builders.

On the occasions that I have climbed the stones that are marked with centuries-old hand impressions, or come upon the unexpected sherd of pottery in a crevice, I have felt the presence of these long-departed souls. Yet, I ask myself, did they really leave, or is the strange feeling that comes over me early in the mornings or late in the evenings still their presence?

The fragrance of sage and juniper that I smell is the same as when they were here. The breeze floating across the mesa murmurs the same soft voice that they once heard. The noonday heat that warmed them warms me also. If I listen with great care, can I hear them singing?

—BEN NIGHTHORSE CAMPBELL

INTRODUCTION

On June 29, 1906, President Theodore Roosevelt signed the act that made Mesa Verde a national park. It was the first, and is still the only, national park in the United States created to preserve archaeological values. Millions of visitors have come from all over the world to see Mesa Verde's beautiful, mysterious cliff dwellings and pueblos. Now, 100 years later, it is only fitting to celebrate the existence of this park, a World Cultural Heritage Site of outstanding universal value.

This anthology marks the centennial and pays tribute to Mesa Verde National Park. In its pages is an examination of the history of an idea: that these archaeological wonders were, and are, worthy of our best efforts to protect them for posterity. Through verbal and visual expression, this book conveys the reactions of the wide diversity of people who explored, founded, developed, and visited Mesa Verde.

In these pages Florence Lister lays the groundwork of the native inhabitants of Mesa Verde, the Ancestral Puebloans, who built the pit houses, pueblos, and cliff dwellings and who made a living here for nearly 800 years. For their descendants, today's southwestern Pueblo people, these sites are still sacred ground.

It should be noted here that history and words used by previous writers do not always match the wishes of modern-day Pueblo people. For example, archaeologists coined the term *Anasazi* for the early inhabitants of the Four Corners. Today, the designation of *Ancestral Puebloan* better indicates the relationship between them and living Pueblo people. References to primitiveness were also sometimes expressed; present sensitivity avoids such judgments and implications. But for the sake of historical accuracy and for what we can learn about past cultural biases, the language in the excerpted material has been left unaltered.

In 1776, European Americans began to leave a written record of this place. The first we have is from Spanish friars Francisco Atanasio Domínguez and Silvestre Velez de Escalante. In that year, they camped along the Dolores and Mancos Rivers at the foot of the mesa but did not come up onto it. In the winter of 1824–1825, trapper William Becknell may have camped within the bounds of what is now the national park.

The first person to leave a definitive record of entry was Dr. John Newberry, geologist on the 1859 Macomb Expedition, who described the mesa's "green slopes and lofty battlements." Following in his footsteps was famed photographer William Henry Jackson, who visited the mesa in 1874 and took the first photograph of a striking cliff dwelling.

After these first few incidental explorations, prospectors and ranchers made more-frequent forays into Mesa Verde. Among them were the Wetherill brothers of Mancos, Colorado, who were soon guiding others into sites such as Spruce Tree House, Cliff Palace, and Balcony House. Also among them was mountaineer

Early corps of park rangers in full dress uniform in Mesa Verde

Large group of visitors poses in Cliff Palace, circa 1920–1930.

Frederick Chapin, who wrote a book in 1892 that cast the national spotlight on Mesa Verde. Soon after, a young Swedish scientist named Gustaf Nordenskiöld was the first to methodically record the mesa's architecture and artifacts.

The year 1893 was a bellwether for Mesa Verde. In that year, Nordenskiöld's classic monograph about the mesa's archaeology was published, and Mesa Verde sites were re-created in miniature for an exhibit at the Chicago World's Columbian Exposition. Most important to the future park was the initiation of a campaign to preserve Mesa Verde. Leading the charge were two women, Virginia McClurg and Lucy Peabody. With their group, the Colorado Cliff Dwellings Association, these women worked tirelessly to convince the public and government officials of the need for preservation. Though a fractious rift developed between McClurg and Peabody, nevertheless it was through their efforts that the United States Congress was convinced to make Mesa Verde a national park.

Even before a National Park Service existed, the necessary steps in developing this park were underway. Boundaries were drawn and land exchanges occurred with the Ute Mountain Ute Indians, who already claimed this part of Colorado. Administrators were hired, and rudimentary visitor accommodations were constructed. Access to the best-known cliff dwellings on Chapin Mesa—Spruce Tree, Cliff Palace, and Balcony House—was a crucial consideration. Various roads were hewn into the steep, unstable slopes from the valley up onto the mesa along which adventuresome early visitors arrived by horse and wagon. Transportation into this remote part of the West would always be a major theme in Mesa Verde's development.

Archaeologists flocked to the new park, including

Though today's highways have smoothed out some of the curves, the land around Mesa Verde has not changed. This map in a 40s era promotional brochure well illustrates that fundamental fact.

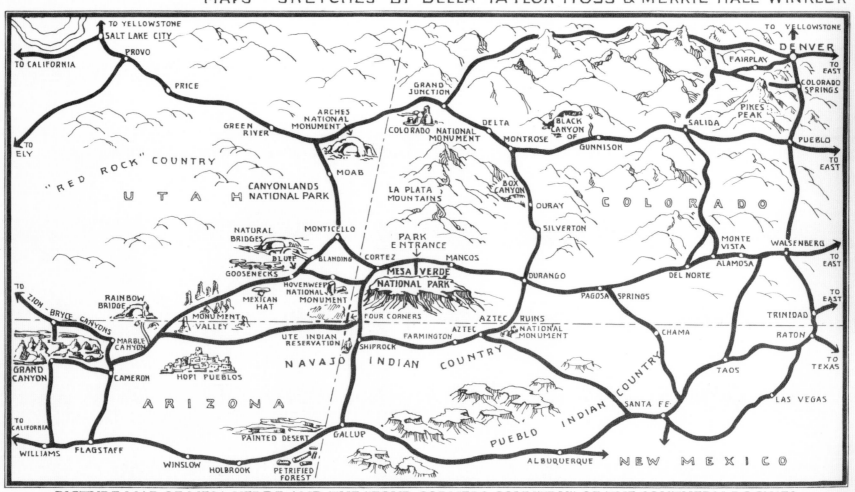

PICTURE MAP OF MESA VERDE AND THE "FOUR-CORNERS COUNTRY" OF THE SOUTHERN ROCKIES

the Smithsonian Institution's Jesse Walter Fewkes, who conducted the earliest excavations. Another Jesse, with the last name Nusbaum, was a contemporary of Fewkes. Nusbaum would serve as superintendent of Mesa Verde for many years and leave a distinct personal imprint on the park.

Mesa Verde's wonders attracted writers and artists too. Author Willa Cather paid a visit in 1915 and wrote an essay that became the foundation of her later novel, *The Professor's House*. Photographer Laura Gilpin rendered the park through the lens of a camera. Contemporary essayist and naturalist Ann Haymond Zwinger, inspired by the park on a similarly intimate level, provides us with a detailed view of Mesa Verde's many treasures.

Through the 1930s, a stronger infrastructure was built with the labor of the depression-era Civilian Conservation Corps. These young men fought fires, built museum exhibits, and stabilized sites. The unyielding concern of Mesa Verde's second fifty years was not how to attract visitors, but how to deal with their growing numbers. After World War II, a mobile public in love with automobiles began arriving, even to this remote corner of the country. Allowing access to the few open cliff dwellings moved the park superintendent in 1956 to bemoan the mass of "milling humanity" that threatened the very values visitors had come to see and explore.

Mesa Verde was suffering serious growing pains. Major additional visitor facilities were erected at Far View under the Mission 66 program. Wetherill Mesa was developed in the 1970s as a way to take pressure off Chapin Mesa's popular sites. Trams began running and ticket systems were put in place. Yet park administrators struggled to find acceptable ways to serve the needs and desires of more than a half million visitors each year while upholding the dual mission of protecting the sites.

Through the 1980s, Mesa Verde's international significance was recognized. Forces that were heedless of park boundaries, such as air pollution, highlighted the need to manage the park's natural, as well as cultural, resources. In 1990 a major piece of federal legislation, the Native American Graves Protection and Repatriation Act, better known as NAGPRA, ushered in a new era of consultation between the park and Native Americans who claim affiliation with it.

In the summers of 2000 and 2002, forest fires burned almost half of the park's land, resetting the clock on fire management and evaluating the effects of this natural force on archaeological sites. And as Colorado historian Duane Smith tells in the epilogue, many of the same challenges that faced Mesa Verde National Park in the first hundred years will remain challenges into the park's second century.

—ROSE HOUK

PROLOGUE
An Essay by Florence Lister

They arrived perhaps 20,000 years ago, walking across the land bridge where the Bering Strait now separates Asia from North America. The exact date when the Paleo-Indian ancestors of the Mesa Verde people migrated will never be known. These early humans depended upon wild game and edible plants for their sustenance and moved about seeking a place where these could best be found. Gradually they drifted southward, separating into various groups isolated by mountains, deserts, and other land and water barriers.

They reached the Mesa Verde region some 2,200 years ago and slowly spread out along the river bottoms, then onto the mesas. For the next thirteen centuries, they would call this place home, evolving from hunter-gatherers into farmers who built villages and migrated no more.

As the sixth century ebbed away, the first permanent settlers arrived on the crest of Mesa Verde. In small family parties they trudged out of the barren high desert to the south, up the sandy bottomlands of the Mancos River drainage, leaving its permanent flow and climbing up to the heights. They looked for cliffside shelters and suitable places for small-scale farming. And they found them.

The massive landform of Mesa Verde, which to early Spanish explorers appeared as a flat green table, actually is shredded by numerous canyons, some 700 to 800 feet deep, that serve as hallways to the south. The mesa bears a thick cap of sandstone through which moisture has percolated down to reach an impervious horizontal layer of dark shale that channels it to the side. Through cycles of freezing and thawing, that water eats away the overburden to form large, arched openings a hundred feet or so below the rimrock. Advance scouts of the straggling bands of sixth-century migrants felt that these places were meant to be homes for some of them. For others, the southern tips of mesa tops offered deep windblown soils for home and garden. With further acquaintance, they would learn that the absence of running water might be compensated for by seeps at the rear of some alcoves and by warmer winters than those of the canyon bottoms.

To archaeologists, these people are known as Modified Basketmakers because of their outstanding skill at that craft. Further material advancement came with the acquisition of pottery-making technology and the bow and arrow to replace spears propelled by atlatls, or shaft levers. These innovations were added to an elaborate inherited tribal wisdom wherein virtually all plants and animals had some use in daily life. Primitive agriculture enhanced that basic wisdom.

Physically the new Mesa Verdeans belonged to a broad grouping of regional Native Americans known as the Southwest Plateau stock ancestral to modern-day Pueblo Indians: short in stature, brown skinned, with straight, coarse, black hair. Although their life spans were generally a brief forty or so years, they were comparable to those of Europeans of the time.

Little is known about their dress. At best, it must have been skimpy. Sandals, breechcloths, aprons of woven fibers, fiber wraps softened with strips of rabbit fur or turkey feathers, and animal hides likely made up their usual clothing. Rare ornaments of shell and stone must have been prized possessions.

The new arrivals settled down and literally dug in. Using pointed sticks, stone axes and mauls, and carrying baskets, each family built its own home. They dug single, shallow, oval-shaped pits to form house walls that were smoothed with mud plaster and roofed with poles, brush, and dirt. The resulting structure resembled a low, brown,

OPPOSITE: *Square Tower House provides a glimpse of the architectural brilliance that marked Mesa Verde's final, and most famous, century of ancestral occupation.*

1

truncated pyramid. Entrance was by means of a ladder through a hole in the roof, which also served as an exit for smoke from a floor-level firepit directly below. There were no interior features other than a few cists for storage, sometimes slabs set on end to define a workspace, and in time a vertical shaft to one side to provide ventilation. The shaft was fronted by an upright stone to keep drafts from extinguishing hearth fires or scattering ashes.

All indoor living—eating, procreating, birthing, sleeping, and reflecting—took place on the ground without benefit of furniture, shelving, or amenities other than animal hides, woven fiber mats, cordage, basketry, and implements of bone, wood, or stone. Combined hearth

earlier. By analogy to the present, scientists believe that it was likely the women who made both. Earthenware had the advantage of withstanding fire, so cookware was born. Lacking a glaze, it leaked, but the oils and grains of its contents helped to seal it. Housekeepers found that they could serve food, cart or dispense liquids so critical in the arid environment, and store dry foods and special objects in various pottery forms.

These pots were obvious beginners' efforts. They were small and often shaped like containers made of other materials. They were formed from clays that baked to a dirty gray color, which deepened to black in smoky cook fires. Most had rounded bottoms so they could be snuggled

2200 B.P.	A.D. 500–600	A.D. 700–800	
Arrival of earliest people to Mesa Verde region.	First Ancestral Puebloans arrive on the Mesa Verde. Erect one-room pithouses in cliff alcoves and on southern tips of mesas. Raise corn, beans, and squash. Hunt with bow and arrows. Acquire pottery-making technology. Weave fiber mats, sandals, aprons, and cordage. Make bone, stone, and shell beads. (Mesa Top Loop, Chapin Mesa; Step House, Wetherill Mesa).	Erect rows of rooms with pole-and-mud walls on ground surface. Retain pithouse as ritual chamber. Subsistence pattern unchanged. Pottery improved with introduction of black-and-white style and more-refined gray utility wares. (Mesa Top Loop, Chapin Mesa).	Erect multiroom sandstone masonry houses. Masonry-lined kiva in front. Larger, more substantial constructions through time. Kivas incorporated into house courtyard. Tunnels. Towers. Introduction of corrugated utility pottery. Black-and-white pottery more elaborate. Check dams on tributaries off mesas. (Mesa Top Loop, Chapin Mesa; Badger House, Wetherill Mesa).

and body heat made such semi-subterranean dwellings snug in winter. In summer the insulating properties of the ground made them cool as caves. These advantages notwithstanding, the pit houses surely were odorous and dark. No wonder most work was done outside, perhaps alongside residents of similar neighboring abodes.

Hand-modeled pottery was an important addition to the inventory of material goods. Although clay receptacles were in some ways vulnerable, they could be fashioned more readily than the baskets that had been ubiquitous

down among supporting hearthstones or held upright in depressions scooped out of earthen floors. Potters decorated some non-cooking vessels with a mineral pigment that blackened with heat. The paint was applied with brushes made of yucca fibers. Crude as it was, this evolving ceramic complex slowly doomed basketry to a secondary status.

One advantage of pottery was that it made possible the consumption of dry beans. At the average 7,000-foot elevation of much of Mesa Verde, trying to parch or boil beans in a basketry tray with hot rocks (the common cooking method of earlier times), was futile. These comestibles needed the long soaking and simmering that pottery afforded. So farmers planted beans in addition to corn and squash. This triad of cultivated food plants—corn, beans, and squash—formed the underpinning of this agrarian society until Spaniards introduced European fruits, vegetables, and domesticated stock in the seventeenth century.

Those Basketmakers who chose the Mesa Verde district as a place to pursue horticulture must have thought it better than where they had come from. Sometimes it was. But at other times, it was too cold, hot, windy, dry, or wet, with a growing season that was too short. There was no perennial water source on the mesa itself to make irrigation possible.

energies involved new basic concepts. Not only did the group have to consider consumption in the present but also saving for the future. There was always the overarching power of amorphous supernatural forces to enrich or destroy. That the people endured in the face of many hardships stands as testimony to their steadfastness.

In the eighth and ninth centuries, an intermediate stage in the local occupation, two changes in the material side of life heralded the Pueblo future. One was new homes being erected on the surface of the mesa tops. Sometimes they were located where former pit dwellings had been, other times in places not previously used. These aboveground dwellings were single rows of four or five rectangular,

A.D. 1100	A.D. 1200– circa 1280	A.D. 1260–1280	A.D. 1276–1299	A.D. 1300	A.D. 1776	A.D 1906
Move to north end of Chapin Mesa. Larger construction, multistory, incorporated kivas, some connected to tunnels. Reservoir for domestic water. (Coyote House, Far View Pueblo; Pipe Shrine House, Chapin Mesa; Badger House, Wetherill Mesa).	Move to cliff alcoves. Erect multi-roomed, multistoried houses, towers, incorporated kivas. Continue to farm on mesa tops. Pottery reaches peak development. (Cliff Palace, Balcony House, Spruce Tree House, Chapin Mesa; Long House, Wetherill Mesa).	Main, late building phase of Cliff Palace.	Great Drought.	Pueblo people gone from Mesa Verde and Four Corners.	First European Americans near Mesa Verde.	Establishment of Mesa Verde National Park

Despite these fundamental drawbacks, these first people of the soil went to work clearing or burning off the dense piñon-juniper forest to create garden plots out beyond their homes. Most evidence of their farms, and any attempt to replenish diminished soil nutrients, has long since vanished. But we can assume that just working the ground without aid of metal tools or draft animals and holding at bay unwanted weeds and voracious animals was a labor-intensive process. Moreover, the whole notion of producing foods through deliberately applied human

flat-roofed, contiguous rooms. Walls were made of vertical poles and brush glued into place by copious mud mortar over irregular slab foundations. A shared wall between two dwellings saved resources and labor. It also reflected the rising communal spirit that still pervades Pueblo thought.

The pit house that once was a dwelling where rituals occasionally took place evolved into a ceremonial chamber, or kiva, that sometimes served domestic purposes. Typically it was sunk to the southeast in front of the line of household rooms, where it and a floor hole opening to the underworld—the *sipapu*—symbolized the people's emergence from the womb of Mother Earth.

The second advancement that can be observed archaeologically was in pottery. It had become indispensable and more varied to meet the needs of the expanding society. Potters learned to coil up larger, more-refined vessels and get them successfully through the critical firing process. A great deal of experimentation in form and decoration is evident. One improvement was the application of a white *engobe*, or slip, over unfired gray pots so that black decorations were highlights. Exteriors of closed-mouth shapes, such as jars or pitchers, were obvious fields for design. However, it was the interior of bowls or ladles that invited decoration, because that was the surface one saw when looking down on objects being used. These early Pueblo designs were edging toward a bold geometric format. Little did the humble Ancestral Puebloan women working in front of their row houses, their hands dirty with clay, know that their black-on-white palette and their design vocabulary would make their vessels unique among all prehistoric ceramics in North America.

During the 900s and 1000s, the cultural momentum and the population grew. In hundreds of scattered settlements on the mesas, sandstone masonry replaced pole-and-mud construction.

Mesa Verde black-on-white double mug, a rare style used in ceremonies

Larger substantial blocks of connected rooms, arranged in squared U- or L-shapes around a central courtyard, became the standard blueprint.

Slowly, to meet the increase in number of residents and perhaps as a response to overexploitation of earlier garden parcels, there was a noticeable movement north along the higher mesa crests, onto the talus slopes, and out into the broader canyon bottoms at the north limits of the mesa. In these locales the soil was thinner, but the precipitation was greater. Workers constructed several reservoirs to catch whatever runoff might be available, perhaps more for domestic use than for agriculture. In all the small drainages cutting down to the Mancos River, farmers built successive lines of unmortared stones across gullies to capture snowmelt, rainwater, and the soils they carried.

Researchers detect subtle clues to mounting fear on Mesa Verde. There was considerable shifting about, some because of exhausted water sources but possibly also because of other concerns. Settlers vacated isolated homes in favor of larger structures housing a number of individuals not necessarily family members. They built thicker walls and stacked up rooms to create several stories. They sealed exterior doors other than those opening to a central courtyard. They brought multiple kivas into the house-block compounds. In addition to shielding chambers from possible attack, these actions suggest religious fervor under stressful conditions. In addition, the Pueblo people raised circular towers several stories tall, some connected to kivas by underground tunnels, some in isolated locales. The motivation of all this drawing inward may have led to the era of the famed cliff dwellings such as Spruce Tree House and Cliff Palace, just as the culture appeared to be reaching a climax.

Excavations in the general region have revealed brutalized human bones that confirm violence disrupting life there during the twelfth and thirteenth centuries. Whether this was a result of cannibalism, warfare, political or social suppression, witchcraft, or some bizarre ritual remains uncertain.

About A.D. 1200, like cliff swallows some Mesa Verdeans began flocking back to the canyon alcoves and ledges where their local history began. In apparent haste, with enormous expenditures of energy, and overcoming the challenges of loose footing on sheer cliffs, they filled more than 600 empty, hard-to-reach spaces along escarpments with masonry constructions. Some were meant for stashed foodstuffs, others as dwellings for people.

The floor plans of domestic structures erected in the overhangs necessarily were dictated by available space, and the buildings obliterated any evidence of former occupation. Included were the customary features of mesa top dwellings such as contiguous rooms, kivas, and towers. Some units were large. For example, Cliff Palace on Chapin Mesa was made up of more than 150 rooms housing perhaps as many as 100 residents. Yet a question has been raised whether this structure was used year-round. Long House on Wetherill Mesa was only slightly smaller.

Though many of the cliff dwellings enjoy a southerly exposure, they must have been demanding places in which to live—cold in winter, cramped and smelly in all seasons, located in rockbound, isolated locations. Their seemingly defensive nature was restricted by lack of secure water sources and ready access.

Not all the men and women on Mesa Verde moved down into the alcoves. Some individuals stayed on the mesa tops. But all continued to depend on farming to provide basic subsistence, which may have been the real threat. When the rains or snows did not fall, the people were in trouble. Scientists have determined that during the late thirteenth century a dry spell turned into a twenty-five-year drought. Stockpiles of foods and seeds for planting were exhausted. Hunger could have promoted strife and thrown lives out of kilter. Probably a package of troubles, including cultural exhaustion, lay behind a slow migration away from the Mesa Verde area that was completed by A.D. 1300. Family by family, clan by clan, the people packed what few articles they could carry on their backs and walked down the canyon hallways that had welcomed their ancestors 750 years before. Upon reaching the Chimney Rock pinnacle that guards the mouth of Mancos Canyon, they dispersed into the San Juan Basin and beyond, out of the Mesa Verde story.

Archaeologists have been able to reconstruct much of the workaday life at Mesa Verde from things left behind. But the intangibles that held life together remain obscure. Because the Ancestral Puebloans had no written language to document their world views, we know nothing of their oral traditions, their songs, their dances, their sacred ceremonies, or the devastating circumstances that drove them away. These imponderables enhance the fascination with them and their spectacular home sites that now draw hundreds of thousands of visitors to the park each year to witness in amazement, and we hope in some spiritual appreciation, their hard-earned achievements.

⊕ FLORENCE LISTER began her career in archaeology at the University of New Mexico in 1939. As a student there, she met and later married southwestern archaeologist Robert (Bob) Lister, with whom she worked for nearly fifty years. With their two sons, Frank and Gary, the Listers lived and worked in national parks and at universities in the West. She coauthored several books with her husband, including *Those Who Came Before: Southwestern Archaeology in the National Park System*, as well as publications on Chaco Canyon, Aztec Ruins, and Earl Morris. Since Robert Lister's death in 1990, Florence has continued to publish works on Four Corners archaeology and leads tours of sites, including Mesa Verde, each summer.

CHAPTER 1

DISCOVERING MESA VERDE:
THE EARLY VISITORS

From the late eighteenth century until Mesa Verde was established as a national park, a variety of Anglo visitors came to look at these mysterious dwellings scattered about southwestern Colorado. Some stumbled on them unexpectedly. Others came with the avowed purpose of seeing them. Many would offer speculations about who had come before, what they had done, and where they had gone.

The mysteries of the cliff dwellings have fascinated people from those days to these. A writer to the April 23, 1881, *Durango Record* thought the "edifices" he had seen "must have been constructed by Aztecs as frontier fortresses." Another report appeared in the September 24 issue of that same newspaper. H. L. Miles and friends, who had just returned from Mancos Canyon and Montezuma Valley, encouraged others to follow in their footsteps as "these curiosities are well worth seeing as tending to show [the architectural skills that] the semi-barbarians of those ancient days attained."

DOMÍNGUEZ AND ESCALANTE

In 1776, two Franciscan priests, Francisco Atanasio Domínguez and Silvestre Velez de Escalante, traveled through southwest Colorado on their way north and west from Santa Fe to the missions of California. In mid-August, the expedition camped along the Mancos River, which they called Rio de San Lazaro, in the shadow of Mesa Verde. The weather was rainy, damp, and cool, and Father Domínguez suffered from a cold and fever. As he got better, they continued on to the Dolores River and made another camp. Although the priests did not enter the mesa itself, the expedition's journal provides us with the earliest written accounts of the Mesa Verde region:

August 12 On the 12th Padre Fray Francisco Atanasio awoke somewhat improved, and more to change terrain and weather than to gain a day's march, we set out from the site and Rio de San Lazaro toward the northwest. We traveled five leagues through leafy tree-growth with good pasturage, took to the west, went two leagues and a half through a sagebrush stretch of little pasturage, and, after a quarter league of travel toward the north, crossed El Rio de Nuestra Senora de Dolores, and halted on its northern edge. ...

August 13 On the 13th we made camp, both to allow the padre to improve some more in order to go ahead, and to take a bearing on the polar elevation of this site and meadow of El Rio de los Dolores, where we found ourselves. The bearing was taken by the sun, and we saw that we were in 380 and 13 ½' latitude. Here there is everything that a good settlement needs for its establishment and maintenance as regards

OPPOSITE: *Mesa Verde National Park, La Plata Mountains in the distance*

Detail from Miera y Pacheco map of Domínguez-Escalante Expedition

Copy of Fray Escalante's journal, in the original Spanish, a document that has proved to be of inestimable value to historians

BACKGROUND: *Miera map from the expedition*

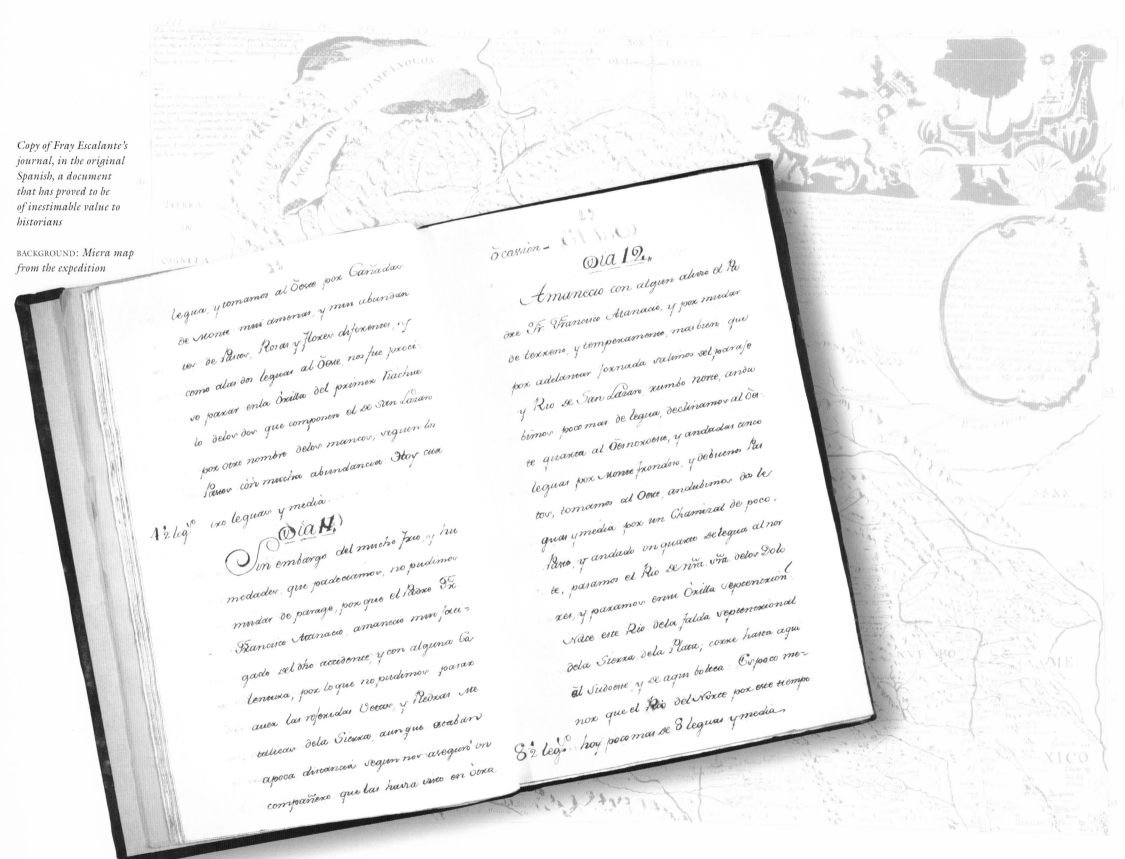

8

irrigable lands, pasturage, timber, and firewood. Upon an elevation on the river's south side, there was in ancient times a small settlement of the same type as those of the Indians of New Mexico, as the ruins which we purposely inspected show. Padre Fray Francisco Atanasio got better, and we decided to continue our journey the following day.

WILLIAM BECKNELL

It would be some time before we had another account of Mesa Verde. In 1824 and 1825 trader William Becknell, the "Father of the Santa Fe Trail," set out with nine men to trap beaver along the Green River. Historians think Becknell's winter quarters were probably made within the boundaries of what is now Mesa Verde National Park. A letter from Mr. Becknell was published in the Franklin, Missouri, *Intelligencer* newspaper on June 25, 1825. In it, he describes the cold, miserable conditions in several feet of snow and their severe hunger, which forced them to eat the flesh and bones of a lean horse and a thin soup made of rawhide. Becknell goes on to tell what they found near their winter camp:

> In the vicinity of our encampment, I discovered old diggings and the remains of furnaces. There are also in this neighborhood the remains of many small stone houses, some of which have one story beneath the surface of the earth. There is likewise an abundance of broken pottery here, well baked and neatly painted. This was probably the site of a town where the ancient Mexican Indians resided, as the Spaniards, who seldom visit this part of the country, can give no account of it. …
>
> As the depth of the snow, and the intense cold of the season rendered trapping almost impracticable, we succeeded, on a third attempt, in making good our retreat from this inhospitable wilderness, and reached a Spanish village … after an absence of five months.

DR. JOHN S. NEWBERRY

With records such as these offering little encouragement, several more decades passed before anyone actually penetrated the formidable wall of Mesa Verde. The person who finally did so was Dr. John S. Newberry, geologist with Capt. J. N. Macomb's expedition. As they moved west from the San Juan Mountains, Newberry describes the sight of the "green slopes and lofty battlements of the Mesa Verde beetling over the plain like some high and rockbound coast above the level ocean."

On August 8, 1859, Dr. Newberry stood atop the mesa on Point Lookout, 8,427 feet above sea level. In literate scientific prose, he paints a picture of the stupendous view of the surrounding landscape: the great expanse of Montezuma Valley covered with stands of sagebrush, the Abajo and La Sal Mountains and Bear's Ears rising to the west in Utah, the San Juan River, and the San Juan Mountains. It is worth noting that Newberry has been credited with naming Mesa Verde, but others say no one knows when or by whom the Spanish name was bestowed. Here is an excerpt from Newberry's report, delayed in publication until 1876 by the Civil War and other obligations:

> To obtain a just conception of the enormous denudation which the Colorado Plateau has suffered, no better point of view could possibly be selected than that of the summit of the Mesa Verde. The geologist here has, as it seems to me, satisfactory proof of the proposition I have before made, that, from the greater portion of the Colorado Plateau, strata more than 2,000 feet in thickness have been removed by erosion. He here has a view toward the west, limited only by the powers of human vision. Directly west the Sage-plain stretches out nearly horizontal, unmarked by any prominent feature, to the distance of a hundred miles. There the island-like mountains, the Sierra Abajo and Sierra La Sal, rise from its surface. South of these is the little doubled-peaked

Color plate of Dolores River and La Plata Mountains, from the Macomb Expedition featured in the Newberry report of 1876

mountain, called by the Mexicans Las Orejas del Oso—the bear's ears; beyond these his vision could not reach, but our explorations enable us to tell him there lies the broad eroded valley of the Colorado, bounded by two steps, of more than 1,000 feet each, below the level of the Sage-plain, and in the bottom of that valley, the chasm of the Colorado Cañon, whose perpendicular walls are 1,500 feet in height; beyond the trough of the Colorado, a plateau corresponding to the Sage-plain, and beyond this a representative of the Mesa Verde. Looking southwest, he would see the Sage-plain terminated in that direction by the excavated valley of the San Juan; beyond this its representatives of similar character

and elevation; higher and more distant than these, the long perspective lines of the lofty mesas north and west of the Moqui villages; the precise counterpart of that on which he is supposed to stand.

WILLIAM HENRY JACKSON

In 1874, frontier photographer William Henry Jackson took the first photograph of a cliff dwelling in the Mesa Verde. Known as Two Story House, it is located on

10

Moccasin Mesa just outside the modern boundaries of Mesa Verde National Park on Ute Mountain Ute Indian lands. As the story goes, around a campfire in the Colorado mountains Jackson learned of the remarkable cliff dwellings on the nearby Mesa Verde. A miner named John Moss was said to be most familiar with the country. As luck would have it, Moss caught up with Jackson as he and a string of hardworking mules jogged along the trail west. A wiry, reserved man addressed as "Captain," Moss obligingly guided Jackson, journalist Ernest Ingersoll, and the mule packers onto the mesa in September 1874. They entered the cliff dwelling as night was falling, and Jackson lugged his heavy view camera back up to make the photograph. Almost a half century later, in a 1924 issue of *The Colorado Magazine*, Jackson recalled the discovery as clearly as if he'd been there only a week ago:

> Our first discovery of a Cliff House that came up to our expectations was made late in the evening of the first day out from Merrit's. We had finished our evening meal of bacon, fresh baked bread and coffee and were standing around the sage brush fire enjoying its genial warmth, with the contented and good natured mood that usually follows a good supper after a day of hard work, and were in a humor to be merry. Looking up at the walls of the canyon that towered above us some 800 to 1,000 feet we commenced bantering Steve, who was a big heavy fellow, about the possibility of having to help carry the boxes up to the top to photograph some ruins up there—with no thought that any were in sight. He asked Moss to point out the particular ruin we had in view; the Captain indicated the highest part of the wall at random. "Yes," said Steve, "I can see it," and sure enough, on closer observation, there was something that looked like a house sandwiched between the strata of the sandstones very near the top. Forgetting the fatigue of the day's work, all hands started out at once to investigate. The first part of the ascent was easy enough, but the upper portion was a perpendicular wall of some 200 feet, and half way up, the cave-like shelf, on which was the little house. Before we had reached the foot of this last cliff only Ingersoll and I remained, the others having seen all they cared for, realizing they would have to do it all over in the morning. It was growing dark, but I wanted to see all there was of it, in order to plan my work for the next day, and Ingersoll remained with me. We were "stumped" for a while in making that last hundred feet, but with the aid of an old dead tree and the remains of some ancient foot holds, we finally reached the bench or platform on which was perched, like a swallow's nest, the "Two Story House" of our first photograph. From this height we had a glorious view over the surrounding canyon walls, while far below our camp fire glimmered in the deepening shadows like a far away little red star.

William Henry Jackson was best known for his photographs, but he also made field sketches, including these of a few sites in the Mesa Verde area.

A year later, Jackson's colleague in the U.S. Geological Survey, William Henry Holmes, visited Mesa Verde. Holmes went into Mancos Canyon in 1875 and 1876, and with what he and Jackson had gathered, assembled clay models of the sites for display at the United States Centennial Exhibition in 1876.

William Henry Jackson took this photograph of Two Story House in September 1874. It is the first known photograph from Mesa Verde.

Together, the photographs and writing of these two explorers opened the eyes of the world to the rich archaeological treasures of Mesa Verde. While people at first knew the place only vicariously through these sources, they found they could actually visit this alluring place once the tracks of the Denver & Rio Grande Railroad were laid to Durango, Colorado, in 1881, only a little more than thirty straight-line miles from the base of the mesa.

8242. Home of the Cliff Dwellers, Columbian Exposition.

LEFT: *The "Home of the Cliff Dwellers," a reconstruction that appeared at the Columbian Exposition in Chicago in 1893*

RIGHT: *Wetherill's Alamo Ranch in Mancos, Colorado*

THE WETHERILLS

Perhaps no other name is more closely associated with Mesa Verde than the Wetherills'. In 1880, Benjamin and Marion Wetherill arrived in the little village of Mancos, Colorado, which then lacked even a post office or a store. The couple soon laid claim to a homestead and built their Alamo Ranch within sight of Mesa Verde. Their five sons—Al, Win, Richard, Clayton, and John—helped develop the ranch and drove cattle along the Mancos River and up onto the plateaus. Pacifist Quakers, the Wetherills

enjoyed good relations with their Ute Indian neighbors. It was a Ute chief who related the existence of a place high up in a canyon that was sacred to them and which they would not enter.

As the story goes, on December 18, 1888, Richard Wetherill and brother-in-law Charles Mason (married to Anna Wetherill) had ridden out to look for stray cows. Through a veil of blowing snow, they looked across the canyon and made out a dwelling tucked into the sandstone cliffs. They had seen cliff dwellings before, but this was the largest and most beautiful. They called it Cliff Palace. The account of the experience is presented by Charlie Mason in a typescript entitled "The Story of the Discovery and Early Exploration of the Cliff Houses at the Mesa Verde," given to the Colorado Historical Society in 1918. The Wetherill brothers signed the manuscript in testimony, all except Richard, who had been killed at Chaco Canyon in June 1910:

In December, 1888, Richard and I went on a cruise of exploration. We followed the Indian trail down Chapin Mesa, between Cliff and Navajo canyons, and camped at the head of a small branch of the Cliff Palace fork of Cliff Cañon. There is a spring of good water in this cañon just under the rimrock. … From the rim of the cañon we had our first view of Cliff Palace just across the cañon from us. To me this is the grandest view of all among the ancient ruins of the Southwest. We rode around the head of the cañon and found a way down

The Wetherill brothers, Al, Win, Richard, Clayton, and John; Charlie Mason's typescript account of his and Richard Wetherill's location of Cliff Palace, signed by the Wetherills

Joists on which floors and roofs were laid had been wrenched out. These timbers are built into the walls and are difficult to remove; even the little willows on which the mud roofs and upper floors are laid, were carefully taken out. No plausable reason for this has been advanced except that it may have been used for fuel. Another strange circumstance is that so many of their valuable possessions were left in the rooms, and covered with the clay of which the roofs and upper floors were made, not to mention many of the walls that were broken down in tearing out the timbers. It would ... that their intention was to conceal their might emies not secure them; or perhaps the people roperty was not considered. There were many as though several people had been killed and lace been abandoned as has been suggested, buildings, all movable articles of value stead of being covered, and much of it rily.

can be no doubt that the Cliff Dwellers savage and warlike neighbors. The men aps adopted into the tribe of the con- migrations may have become necessary from outside tribes.

John Wetherill
Kayenta
Arizona

Clayton Wetherill
Creede Colo

Richard Wetherill killed by
Navajo at Pueblo Bonito N.M.
June 22nd 1910

B. A. Wetherill
Mannelito N.Mex

Al Wetherill
Ganado
Arizona

C. C. Mason
Hermit
Colo

over the cliffs to the level of the building. We spent several hours going from room to room, and picked up several articles of interest, among them a stone axe with the handle still on it. There were also parts of several human skeletons scattered about. A year or more before this Al had seen Cliff Palace, but did not enter it; he was on his way to camp after a long tramp on foot, and was very tired, he was following the bottom of the cañon and only got a partial view so did not climb up, and it remained for Richard and I to be the first to explore the building.

The story of Richard Wetherill and Charlie Mason's Cliff Palace discovery has been told so often it has become fixed as legend. But other Anglo-Americans made claims to having found Cliff Palace earlier, including Al Wetherill, as Mason mentions; miner John Barlow Frasher; a man with a government surveying party named Chapman Ballard; and local rancher James Frink. Another was prospector S. E. Osborn, who penned an article for a Denver newspaper of his activities in Mesa Verde during the winter of 1883–1884. Osborn claimed to have entered several structures, possibly including Balcony House and Cliff Palace, and he left tangible evidence of his presence by scratching his name and the date, March 20, 1884, on a boulder in a cliff dwelling.

According to historian David Harrell, all of these claims regarding Cliff Palace either conflict, are poorly documented, or lack positive confirmation. And, as Harrell points out, when all is said and done it is not so important who saw Cliff Palace first. "Even if Wetherill and Mason were not the first to see Cliff Palace," he writes, "they were the first to reveal it."

The Wetherills revealed many other sites in Mesa Verde over the next two decades, and they proceeded to excavate the sites, guide others to them, and make a substantial collection of artifacts. The Wetherills' efforts to interest the Smithsonian Institution and other museums in acquiring these holdings were largely futile. The Colorado Historical Society did purchase one collection from them, reportedly for $3,000, though this remains an issue of debate.

Although such a transaction today would spark loud protest, in those days it was acceptable and fully legal. And there were benefits to the purchase of objects from Mesa Verde: the impressive collection remained intact and accessible to scientists and the public who visited the Colorado State Museum in Denver. A second Wetherill collection was exhibited in Durango, Pueblo, Denver, and finally at the Chicago World's Fair in 1893.

The Wetherills were among the first voices to call for preservation of Mesa Verde as a national park.

FREDERICK CHAPIN

Around this same time, in 1889 and 1890, Richard Wetherill guided author and mountaineer Frederick Chapin into Mesa Verde. During his two summers of exploration, Chapin used pack stock to pioneer several different routes up onto the mesa. Chapin then wrote a book, *The Land of the Cliff Dwellers*, published in 1892. Widely distributed, the book was read by people all over the country. *The Land of the Cliff Dwellers* was the first popular work on Mesa Verde, and it drew the attention of the entire nation and beyond. It is for Frederick Chapin, incidentally, that Chapin Mesa was named, where the park museum and headquarters are now located.

In the last chapter of his book, Chapin describes a day on Mesa Verde and concludes with his own speculations about how the early people subsisted and what happened to them:

> Let me finally describe one of our journeys across the Mesa. Our camp was on the brink of Cliff Cañon. We reached it long after dark; and after the usual hard riding

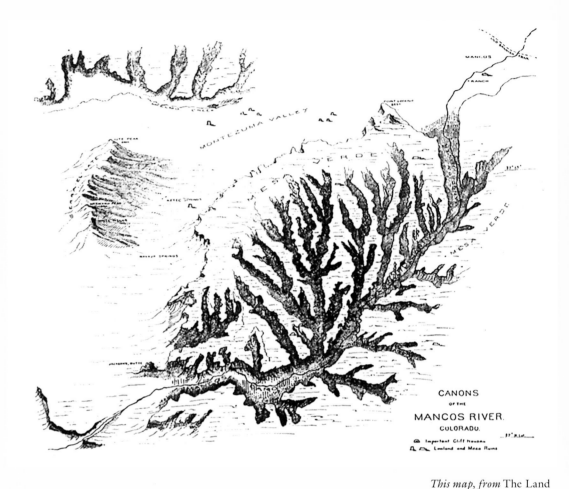

This map, from The Land of the Cliff Dwellers, *clearly shows how canyons finger down off the Mesa Verde to the Mancos River.*

after stray horses, we got everything to rights and whiled away the evening hours by a huge fire. …

The next morning dawned warm and bright, with a pleasant light breeze. We were up at sunrise, and off at eight o'clock, delaying only to photograph the camp and pack-animals. Our route lay to the north, along the mesa summit, and between Cliff and Navajo Cañons, which here run nearly parallel with the main one. We passed near the ends of many tributaries of these gorges, which showed that while it was a comparatively easy matter to get out of this country to the north, to come back to any given point from that direction would be impossible to any one not familiar with all the arms of the different cañons. …

We observed no traces of ancient roads on the Mesa, nor of irrigating ditches; but we passed the ruins of what appears to have been a large reservoir. …

All the morning we followed trails leading through the extensive chaparral of juniper and piñon trees. The piñons were loaded with nuts, which are good eating. The Indians make flour from them … flying about were many piñon birds. The trails were made by Indians, deer, or cattle. …

About noon we reached the summit of the Mesa. … A most remarkable view was unfolded. … Here, within sight of our valley, and within a few hours' ride of it, we were able to while away the midday hours, and—as perhaps the former inhabitants of this strange land may have done at this same outlook—watch the panorama. …

Looking over the wide stretch of country, we recalled the fact that to the early explorers this land seemed a desert. And well indeed it might. Over the wide arid plains stretch miles of waste acres covered with sage-brush and grease-wood. Yet all along the tops of the great Mesa over which we had been riding, pottery is strewn and signs of a primitive race are found. Its numbers must have been large, or the period of their stay prolonged.

It has been inferred by some writers that there must formerly have been a greater annual rainfall, in order that such a population could have been supported by agricultural employment; but judging from so much evidence that we found in the way of tanks and fragments of large water-jars, it would appear that the country was lacking in water even when occupied by the Cliff-Dwellers. And the hypothesis of a change of climate therefore becomes unnecessary. That the vanished race could have gained subsistence by tillage of the soil, seems evidenced by what the farmers of Mancos and Montezuma Valleys are doing; … and the time may come when the land … will be overturned and tilled, and all along the broad tablelands and in many of the fertile cañon beds we shall see the tasselled maize bend, and fields of wheat wave to the breeze. Then it will no longer seem incredible when we read that the country once supported a great population, a people well advanced in many arts, and who conceived of certain forms of beauty. … And may we not imagine them a race who loved peace rather than war, but who, hard pressed by a savage foe, fought stubbornly and long, and died rather than desert their romantic fortresses among the cañon cliffs?

Gustaf Nordenskiöld, intrepid Swedish dilettante and early investigator of Mesa Verde.

GUSTAF NORDENSKIÖLD

A twenty-two-year-old graduate from the University of Uppsala in Sweden, Gustaf Nordenskiöld came to the western United States in 1891 seeking recovery from tuberculosis. Upon his arrival in Denver, Nordenskiöld met botanist Alice Eastwood, who provided him with a letter of introduction to the Wetherill family. He went immediately to the family's Alamo Ranch in Mancos, planning to stay only a week. Instead, counter to his father's wishes, Nordenskiöld spent the rest of the summer working at major sites both on Chapin Mesa and Wetherill Mesa.

Until October, Nordenskiöld used a Kodak camera for his photographs; then his large-view camera with glass plate negatives arrived, and he returned to photograph and map the sites.

When Nordenskiöld tried to ship his Mesa Verde collections back to Sweden, he was arrested at midnight in the Strater Hotel in Durango, Colorado. In the ensuing uproar, he was accused by the public and the press of outright looting. The complaint against him, however, was quickly dismissed because no laws at that time prohibited such collections or shipments. The bulk of Nordenskiöld's collection, close to 700 items, eventually ended up in the holdings of the National Museum of Finland in Helsinki.

Nordenskiöld's investigations were a notch above the casual and incidental digging and collecting that had been taking place. His field notes, maps, and photographs of Mesa Verde sites were meticulous and of high quality.

But Gustaf Nordenskiöld did not live long enough to return to Mesa Verde. His health worsened and he died on

Nordenskiöld's photograph of Cliff Palace, taken in 1891

June 5, 1895, at age twenty-six, leaving behind a wife and young daughter.

He did, however, live to see publication of his landmark monograph, *The Cliff Dwellers of Mesa Verde, Southwestern Colorado: Their Pottery and Implements.* It was written first in Swedish and then translated into English, and still stands as the first true scientific work on some of Mesa Verde's finest cliff dwellings. In this excerpt, when Nordenskiöld locates and enters Spring House, we sense the excitement of discovery he experienced almost daily during his summer at Mesa Verde:

> On following the edge of Wetherill's Mesa from Step House a few hundred paces to the south or south-east, we descry in the opposite wall of the cañon an extensive cliff-dwelling, Spring House. What a striking view these ruins present at a distance! The explorer pictures to himself a whole town in miniature under the lofty vault of rock in the cliff before him. But the town is a deserted one: not a sound breaks the silence, and not a movement meets the eye, among those gloomy, half ruined walls, whose contours stand off sharply from the darkness of the inner cave. Spring House is situated high up the wall of the cañon, and both below and above the ruin the rocks are very steep. …

> This ruin has been called Spring House from a spring situated at the back of the cave. … Two slender, quadrangular pillars of sandstone have been erected here to support an extensive roof. It seems to have been customary in the construction of these buildings always to leave an open space behind the whole cliff-dwelling. In order to provide support for the floor of an upper story, without having to encroach upon this space by building walls, the builders have erected these pillars. …

> Spring House is fairly well protected from attack by its site. From the bottom of the cañon the buildings can be reached only by a difficult and dangerous climb from ledge to ledge; and a very circuitous route, either up or down the cañon, must be taken to scale the mesa from the ruin. …

> What can have induced a people to have recourse to dwelling-places so incommodious? This is a question that has undoubtedly suggested itself many times already to the reader. The answer must be, that nothing short of the ever imminent attacks of a hostile people, can have driven the cliff-dwellers to these impregnable mountain fastnesses, which afforded a safe refuge, so long as food and water held out.

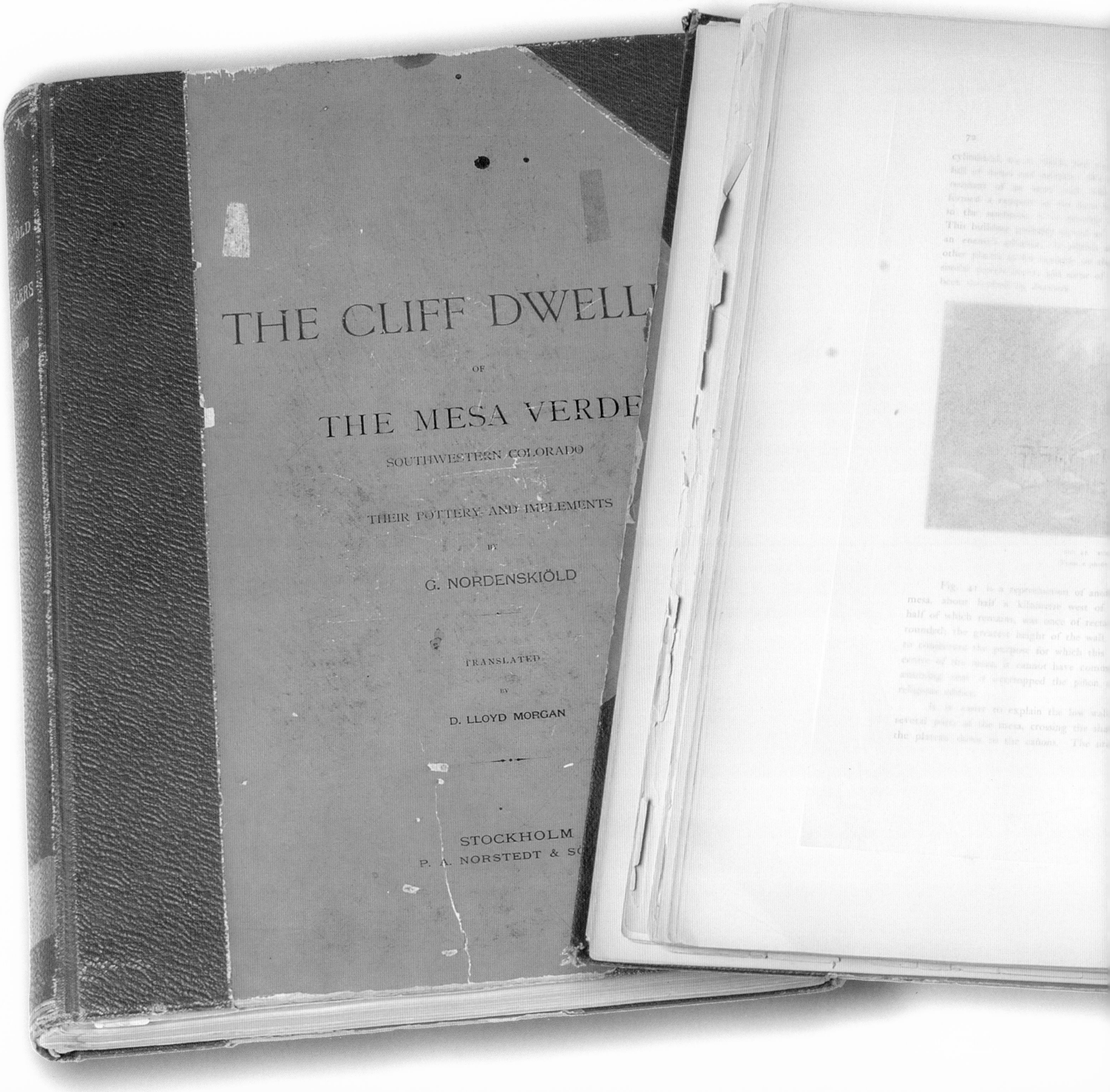

Nordenskiöld's classic monograph, The Cliff Dwellers of the Mesa Verde, *held great significance in revealing Mesa Verde to the larger world.*

THE CLIFF DWELLE

OF

THE MESA VERDE

SOUTHWESTERN COLORADO

THEIR POTTERY AND IMPLEMENTS

BY

G. NORDENSKIÖLD

TRANSLATED

BY

D. LLOYD MORGAN

STOCKHOLM
P. A. NORSTEDT & SÖ

G. Nordenskiöld: The Cliff Dwellers of the Mesa Verde.   XVI

Ruins of a tower in Navajo Cañon.
From a photograph by the author.

CHAPTER 2

ESTABLISHING A NATIONAL PARK

Right from the start, visitors began taking home souvenirs of their visits to these ancient sites. As early as the 1870s, settlers moving into the Animas and Mancos river valleys gathered relics. Denver's *Rocky Mountain News* (November 25, 1877) reported that one farmer, identified only as Tripp, "has a large collection of relics." The first account of people scratching their names in the old dwellings appeared in 1878.

In the eyes of that generation, there seemed nothing wrong with this. People had been vandalizing ancient sites since time immemorial. It took farsighted individuals to see that much was being lost as people dug through these dwellings and found souvenirs that ended up in places unknown. Fortunately, there appeared those who strongly believed that this cultural heritage was worth preserving, many of them women, and they were willing to take a stand before it was too late.

THE WOMEN'S PARK

Eighteen ninety-three was a watershed year for Mesa Verde. Not only was Gustaf Nordenskiöld's monograph published in that year, collections from Mesa Verde were displayed at the Chicago World's Columbian Exposition. Fairgoers were fascinated by the miniature re-creations of Cliff Palace, Square Tower House, and Balcony House.

Also in 1893, Virginia Donaghe McClurg launched her campaign to preserve Mesa Verde. As a correspondent for the *New York Graphic* before her marriage, Virginia Donaghe had first visited Mesa Verde a decade earlier, in 1884, under cavalry escort. She returned in 1886, married Gilbert McClurg three years later, and settled in Colorado Springs. Increasing publicity about Mesa Verde, and rampant pothunting by locals who were hard-pressed by the 1893 depression, led to further destruction of sites and removal of irreplaceable archaeological material. This situation sparked McClurg's efforts to see a park established.

She enlisted the support of the Colorado Federation of Women's Clubs, published articles and poems, and wrote letters to people in high places, including Presidents William McKinley and Theodore Roosevelt. McClurg also lectured widely: in 1894, a one-dollar season ticket admitted members of the Ladies' Aid Society in Denver to her four talks on "The Pre-Historic Southwest." She approached the Ute Indians, who then lived on and claimed the land, with the idea of a lease. In exchange, the Utes would vacate the land where the cliff dwellings were located. When Ute chief Ignacio requested more money than she could afford, McClurg demurred. It was then that she stated her determination to "let this be the women's park."

With others at her side, including Lucy Peabody, a

OPPOSITE: *Balcony House was for many years a focus of the Colorado Cliff Dwellings Association.*

THE MESA VERDE CLIFF DWELLINGS

AND THE WOMEN'S PARK.

By VIRGINIA DONAGHE M'CLURG,

Chairman of the Committee for the Preservation and Restoration of the Cliff and Pueblo Ruins of Colorado.

CLIFF DWELLERS' POTTERY.
(From Mrs. McClurg's Collection.)

VIRGINIA DONAGHE M'CLURG.

THE MANCOS BROWN STONE FRONT.

A DEGENERATE CLIFF DWELLER.
(From Mrs. McClurg's Collection.)

woman well connected politically to powerful people in Washington, D.C., McClurg founded the Colorado Cliff Dwellings Association in 1900. Lucy Peabody led the effort in the nation's capital as bills were introduced in Congress from 1900 through 1905. They all failed. Meanwhile, under McClurg's zealous leadership, the women continued to raise money and sponsor tours of Mesa Verde for influential members of the national press and others, among them Smithsonian archaeologist Jesse Walter Fewkes.

In 1906, with conservationist Theodore Roosevelt as president, political climate and public sentiment finally were ripe to achieve the Cliff Dwellings Association's goals. Unfortunately, at this critical juncture, a large rift opened between the two most influential supporters. Virginia McClurg wanted a state park under control of the women's group and withdrew her support for a national park at the last hour, while Lucy Peabody maintained her staunch support for a national park. News of the rift hit the press, and emotions ran high. Nevertheless, legislation creating Mesa Verde National Park passed Congress and was signed by the president on June 29, 1906. Mesa Verde was the nation's first park set aside for archaeological resources. (Today it remains the country's only archaeological national park, though there are many national monuments and historical parks set aside for that reason.)

In the aftermath, Lucy Peabody earned the accolade "Mother of Mesa Verde National Park." Yet Virginia McClurg maintained her interest and involvement in the park by funding Fewkes's excavations of Balcony House in 1908 and continuing to correspond through the 1920s with government officials, including then–park superintendent Jesse Nusbaum. She pressed for some kind of plaque or exhibit at Balcony House memorializing the work of the Colorado Cliff Dwellings Association, but a plaque was never installed.

The Mesa Verde National Park.

MRS. W. S. PEABODY.

SOME philosopher who knew the ways of the human heart, Emerson, I think, said that people would, at great expense of time and money, spend years of travel abroad, and then come home to find interests in their own dooryards which gave them as much pleasure as the Leaning Tower at Pisa, or the ruins of the Roman Acropolis.

can continent was inhabited by a people who have never yet been linked, either by science or history, with the peoples which came after them.

In the Mesa Verde National Park this state has something of which to be proud. Not only is the park of interest because of its large scientific value, but it means much to the state in the thous-

MRS. W. S. PEABODY
The "Mother" of the Mesa Verde
National Park.

PROFESSOR
EDGAR L. HEWETT
Director of American
Archaeology in the
Archaeological Institute
of America.

MAJOR H. M. RANDOLPH
Superintendent of the Mesa Verde
National Park.

Down in southwestern Colorado, in canons that, until a comparatively recent period, have been accessible only to the coyotes and eagles, there have slumbered for aeons the remnants of a lost civilization. By the creation of the Mesa Verde National Park, the wonderful ruins of the ancient cliff dwellers are not only to be preserved for the future, but it is hoped that some of the secrets of the past may be unlocked, and light thrown upon the period when the Ameri-

ands of people and the hundreds of thousands of dollars it will annually bring within her borders. Colorado should lend every assistance possible to the national government in the development of this park. In planning for their next summer's vacation, all loyal Coloradoans should turn their backs upon the seductive watering places of the East or the attractions of Europe, and decide to fill a traveling bag with "old clothes" and take an out-

OPPOSITE: *Virginia McClurg, cofounder of the group that helped save Mesa Verde's antiquities, was a prolific promoter of the park idea.*

Lucy Peabody's article in The Modern World, *1907, heralded the wonders of Mesa Verde National Park.*

The October 1907 issue of *Modern World* magazine included an article entitled "The Mesa Verde National Park," with the byline of Mrs. W. S. Peabody. In the article Lucy Peabody extols the new park, describes the attractions, and trumpets its potential value to Colorado's economy. Indeed, in her mind it was a patriotic duty of citizens to visit the park.

As the writings show, the link between modern Puebloan people and their ancestors in Mesa Verde was not known to Mrs. Peabody and others of her time:

Down in southwestern Colorado, in cañons that, until a comparatively recent period, have been accessible only to the coyotes and eagles, there have slumbered for aeons the remnants of a lost civilization. By the creation of the Mesa Verde National Park, the wonderful ruins of the ancient cliff dwellers are not only to be preserved for the future, but it is hoped that some of the secrets of the past may be unlocked, and light thrown upon the period when the American continent was inhabited by a people who have never yet been linked, either by science or history, with the peoples which came after them.

In the Mesa Verde National Park this state has something of which to be proud. Not only is the park of interest because of its large scientific value, but it means much to the state in the thousands of people and the hundreds of dollars it will annually bring within her borders. Colorado should lend every assistance possible to the national government in the development of this park. In planning for their next summer's vacation, all loyal Coloradoans should turn their backs upon the seductive watering places of the East or the attractions of Europe, and decide to fill a traveling bag with "old clothes" and take an outing in this newest and most unique of the national parks. If they do, they can count on receiving benefit in three ways: in learning something fur-

W hen Lucy Peabody won the battle about state versus federal oversite (she wanted federal oversite for Mesa Verde), Virginia McClurg went home and helped create Manitou Springs.

A reproduction of a Mesa Verde cliff dwelling was constructed in a canyon at Manitou Springs, Colorado, by an entrepreneur who brought in stones from several Four Corners archaeological sites. The replica opened to tourists about the same time that Mesa Verde was established as a national park. Promoted as scientific and authentic, the place bothered park superintendent Jesse Nusbaum, who deplored the "constant 'bally-hoo'" about it. In the 1960s, the faux dwelling was touted in travel publications as "dating from approximately 1019 A.D." A modern Web site still advertises, "authentic Anasazi cliff dwellings, built more than 700 years ago." The entrance is designed to mimic the entrance of a national park, right down to the entrance kiosks and flags.

ther about the resources of their own state; in spending their money at home, and also in becoming acquainted with some of the oldest works of prehistoric man that are to be found anywhere on the globe.

In the July 1916 *TRAVEL* magazine, Gilbert and Virginia McClurg contributed an article titled "The Development of the Mesa Verde National Park." The authors describe the park's big summer event that year, a pageant to celebrate the jubilee of the Colorado Cliff Dwellings Association. The lengthy article (written in third person) goes on to detail the features of Mesa Verde, the history of its Pueblo inhabitants, Anglo-American discovery, and establishment as a national park, especially the efforts of Mrs. McClurg and the Colorado Cliff Dwellings Association.

Although Mrs. McClurg's first attempt to secure a lease with the Utes failed, a lease was successfully completed later.

The Colorado Cliff Dwellings' Association—that patient and persevering body of two hundred women which has unselfishly labored for a quarter of a century to save Mesa Verde, Colorado, and its ancient cliff dwellings as a National Park—is to celebrate in late August its year of jubilee. A memorial tablet is to be unveiled, and from the Atlantic to the Pacific guests are coming by railway or motor car to see a novel pantomime pageant staged in the very ruins themselves. The footlights will be blazing piles of piñon wood, and by this illumination an old Pueblo Indian legend dramatized, "The Marriage of the Dawn and the Moon" ... The banquet will be as novel as the play. Relying upon the resources of the land, with a suggestion of the viands approved by the cliff dwellers of old, the ladies of the Association will have a barbecue for all who come. Roast calves and sheep will turn upon the spit, and baked ears of maize and trays of peaches will recall Indian staples of the region. Water will be supplied from Hammond Spring, a source of water supply known to the ancient inhabitants and developed at the expense of Mrs. John Hays Hammond, one of the members

of the Colorado Cliff Dwellings' Association. ...

The work of the Colorado Cliff Dwellings' Association has included:

The first practical map of Mesa Verde, made at the instance and expense of the Association; the first wagon road through the cañon; the trip of anthropologists to Mesa Verde (September 4 to 7, 1901) as guests of the Association; also trips to the Mesa Verde of men prominent in political life on other occasions; the development of Hammond Spring at Spruce Tree House at an expense of several hundred dollars; a lease from the Weeminuche Utes for the land on which the ruins stand, devised and paid for (as temporary means of protection from squatters, cattle-grazers and relic-hunters); the repairing of Balcony House; unceasing propaganda (by means of illustrated lectures, pictures, books, Indian music, relic displays ...) to stimulate interest in Indian life in general and the Pueblo Indian in particular.

Through the direct influence of the Association, Congress passed bills to sanction the Indian lease; to establish a commission to treat with the Utes for the cession of Mesa Verde; to appropriate a little less than $1,000 to survey Mesa Verde; to amend the Hogg bill, withdrawing the cliff ruins of Mesa Verde for park purposes, and to appropriate $7,500 for the maintenance of Mesa Verde National Park.

THE LEGISLATION

Creation of the new national park meant that the federal government had to deal with the issue of Ute claims to the land. In 1903, the U.S. Congress authorized negotiations with the Utes, and an agreement was ratified in 1906. A land swap was agreed to in 1913, with the Utes receiving acreage on Ute Mountain in exchange for land in Mesa Verde.

The park's founding legislation, passed by the 59th Congress on June 29, 1906, and signed by President Theodore Roosevelt, spelled out the park boundaries in detail:

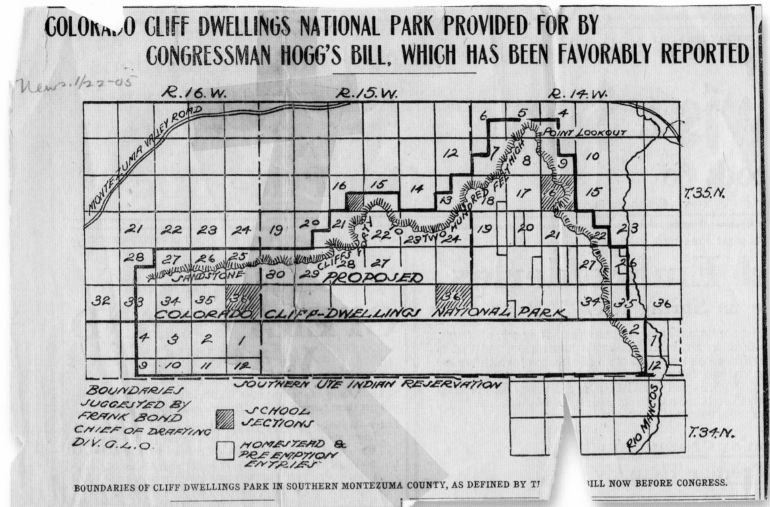

The Colorado Cliff Dwellings Association paid for surveying and mapping to accompany the bill in the U.S. Congress to create Mesa Verde National Park. Boundaries changed when the park was actually established.

'A resolution was adopted at the annual meeting of the State Historical society Tuesday night indorsing the bill now before congress making the Mesa Verde National park out of the southwestern corner of Montezuma county in southern Colorado, which includes all the principal ruins left by the cliff dwellers. The bill is meeting with popular indorsement throughout the state, and, with the approval of the committee on public lands and the secretary of the interior, is practically assured of passage. Congressman Hogg is to father the bill in the house and Senator Patterson will introduce it in the senate.

Although the Colorado Cliff Dwellings association has been working for five years to secure the passage of an act making the territory including the more important ruins public property, it has continually been disappointed until last week. Its first efforts were bent toward having the state purchase the property and convert it into a state park, but this was found to be impossible, and since then efforts have been centered in Washington. While Speaker Henderson was at the head of the house his hostility to the bill made it impossible to proceed with it, and the opposition of the secretary of the interior, which has been overcome by the proof of good surveys, was another stumbling block in the way of the archeolog-ical associations which tried so long to insure the preservation of the ruins and castles of the early cliff dwellers.

Section 3 of the Hogg bill permits the secretary of the interior to allow reputable museums and scientific schools to conduct examinations of the ruins, subject to the rules he may prescribe.

Section 4 is the penalty clause of the act. It provides a fine of $1 to $1,000 and imprisonment from one to twelve months for persons committing vandalism in the park.

DENVER LANDMARK MAKES WAY FOR BUSINESS BLOCK

Another Denver landmark is a thing of the past. Yesterday workmen tore down a little log cabin 16x18 feet at 1424 Market street to make way for a two-story business building. The new improvement will be owned by J. E. Button, the Fifteenth street creamery man.

Architect Frank S. Snell prepared the plans and took out a building permit last Friday. The improvement will cost $10,-000, and provision will be made for an additional story at any time.

The cabin demolished is said to have been one of the oldest abodes in Denver. For months past it has been hidden from view by a large theatrical billboard. The property on which the cabin stood was purchased by Mr. Button for about $1,500.

Sec. 2. That said public park shall be known as the Mesa Verde National Park, and shall be under the exclusive control of the Secretary of the Interior, whose duty it shall be to prescribe such rules and regulations and establish such service as he may deem necessary for the care and management of the same. Such regulations shall provide specifically for the preservation from injury or spoliation of the ruins and other works and relics of prehistoric or primitive man within said park: Provided, That all prehistoric ruins that are situated within five miles of the boundaries of said park, as herein described, on Indian lands and not on lands alienated by patent from the ownership of the United States, are hereby placed under the custodianship of the Secretary of the Interior, and shall be administered by the same service that is established for the custodianship of the park. [This provision was necessary because, as originally established, the land included in the park failed to encompass most of the main archaeological sites.]

Sec. 3. That the Secretary of the Interior be, and he is hereby, authorized to permit examinations, excavations, and other gathering of objects of interest within said park by any person or persons whom he may deem properly qualified to conduct such examinations, excavations, or gatherings, subject to such rules and regulations as he may prescribe: Provided always, That the examinations, excavations, and gatherings are undertaken only for the benefit of some reputable museum, university, college, or other recognized scientific or educational institution, with a view to increasing the knowledge of such objects and aiding the general advancement of archaeological science.

Sec. 4. That any person or persons who may otherwise in any manner willfully remove, disturb, destroy, or molest any of the ruins, mounds, buildings, graves, relics, or other evidences of an ancient civilization or other property from said park shall be deemed guilty of a misdemeanor, and upon conviction before any court having jurisdiction of such offenses shall be fined not more than one thousand dollars or imprisoned not more than twelve months, or such person or persons may be fined and imprisoned, at the discretion of the judge, and shall be required to restore the property disturbed, if possible.

SURVEYING THE PARK AND OTHER ADMINISTRATIVE MATTERS

With the park's establishment, eminent archaeologist Edgar Lee Hewett, one of the authors of the park's founding legislation, was employed by the Smithsonian Institution to help survey the park's boundaries. In his "Report on the Ruins of Mesa Verde, Colorado," Hewett gave his opinion of the sites he felt were of greatest interest to visitors and the sites' state of preservation at the time they came into the government's hands:

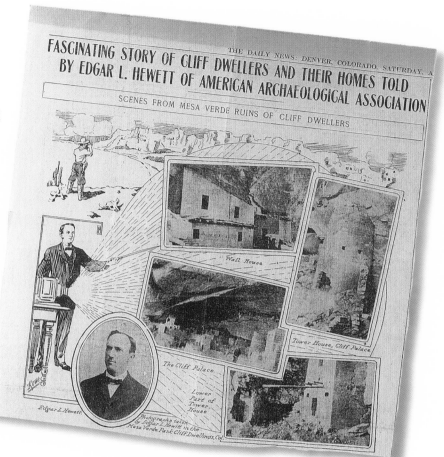

Archaeologist Edgar Hewett helped promote Mesa Verde to the Denver public, and portrayed his multiple roles on a page of The Daily News.

The ruins on the Mesa Verde are the most noteworthy group of prehistoric buildings within the limits of the United States. They are the finest existing specimens of the general class of ancient structures known as cliff dwellings. They occupy natural recesses in the cañon walls, from 500 to 1000 feet above the dry creek beds. Some of these caverns are small, almost inaccessible and contain houses of from one to a dozen rooms. Of these the number within the jurisdiction of the park will reach into hundreds. A number of large commodious caverns contain assemblages of dwellings attaining to the magnitude of towns. …

The cañons that are richest in ruins are the Mancos, Cliff and Navajo. It is these that most will wish to explore. …

The most conspicuous of the large cliff villages are three known as Cliff Palace, Sprucetree House and Balcony House, all situated within a radius of two miles of one another. These are the ruins that will be visited by all travelers who go to the park. The three can be reached and inspected comfortably in a day's visit. It will be only the exceptional student that will care to assay the arduous task of reaching the smaller and more remote dwellings. ...

The cliff dwellings have withstood remarkably well the various destructive agencies that have operated against them. They are monuments to the skill of their primitive builders. They are advantageously situated for protection, being difficult of access and mostly under huge overhanging ledges of the rim rock of the plateau which shields them from the weather. Were it not for man's destructiveness, they would probably exist today in about the state in which they were left by their builders. Unfortunately, they have been the prey of treasure-hunters and unscientific collectors for many years, and have suffered irreparable damage. Many important structures have been completely demolished and in many cases walls partially destroyed and left in conditions for fur-

ther rapid deterioration. There is need for immediate repairs in Cliff Palace, Sprucetree House and Balcony House to prevent the falling of walls that have been left unsupported. The ruins are full of debris, which should be carefully removed. ... While the dwellings have for the most part been looted of their contents, it is probable that much valuable material may still be recovered.

Hewett further recommended that Cliff Palace should be the first site restored, that a superintendent be hired and live in the park during prime tourist season, and that a wagon road be improved into the park. These and other administrative matters would begin to absorb all the attention and funding for the new national park.

The first permanent superintendent was Hans Randolph, officer in the Colorado State Militia and a friend of Lucy Peabody. Randolph set up an office in Mancos and then tried to rid Spruce Tree Camp of trash, build a wagon road up to the park, repair archaeological sites, install a telephone line, and build a reservoir to assure a water supply. He hired veteran guide Charles Kelly as the park's first permanent ranger. After four years on the job, Randolph was out in 1911, and Kelly went back to working full-time as a private guide.

Over the next ten years, Mesa Verde would have four other acting or permanent superintendents, most of whom were political appointments. All continued the fundamental tasks begun by their predecessors, some more ably than others.

A political cartoon of the day conveys the thought that the federal government would be the better agent to take care of Mesa Verde.

MISS COLORADO: "THEY'LL BE SAFER IN YOUR CARE, UNCLE!"

The first park headquarters were located outside the park itself, in a bank building in the town of Mancos. Acting park superintendent Richard Wright is shown there in 1911.

CHAPTER 3

DIGGING INTO THE PAST: ARCHAEOLOGY

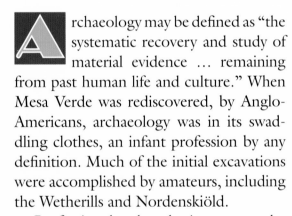

Archaeology may be defined as "the systematic recovery and study of material evidence … remaining from past human life and culture." When Mesa Verde was rediscovered, by Anglo-Americans, archaeology was in its swaddling clothes, an infant profession by any definition. Much of the initial excavations were accomplished by amateurs, including the Wetherills and Nordenskiöld.

Professional archaeologists appeared on the scene with the new century, and with them came a more systematic study of Mesa Verde. Granted their methods now appear primitive, but the movement they started has evolved over the last 100 years. It is an ongoing race to preserve Mesa Verde's heritage against onrushing civilization, crowds, and changing times. New techniques and methods allow fresh interpretations of the past, continually beckoning new studies and adding to our knowledge of the Ancestral Puebloan culture.

CONNECTING MODERN-DAY AND ANCESTRAL PUEBLOANS: JESSE WALTER FEWKES

The era of amateur archaeology and pothunting at Mesa Verde came to an end in 1908, with the arrival of

Jesse Walter Fewkes of the Smithsonian's Bureau of American Ethnology. Fewkes, then in his sixties, set about excavating and stabilizing sites to make them safe for public visitation. In his first season in the park, in 1908, he worked in Spruce Tree House, the following year at Cliff Palace, and later years through 1922 at Sun Temple, Far View, and others—fifteen field seasons in all at Mesa Verde.

In 1915, Jesse Walter Fewkes initiated what would become a beloved park service tradition—evening campfire talks for visitors. He also lectured in the park's first museum, a log cabin on Chapin Mesa. Fewkes's excavations still stand as baseline information for several major sites at Mesa Verde.

Fewkes has been criticized for his lack of scientific rigor, and many do not attribute much lasting value to his archaeological work. As an ethnologist, his abiding interest was recording the oral histories of Indian groups, especially the Hopi. Fewkes was given to comparing modern-day Pueblos to the earlier people who lived at Mesa Verde, making questionable leaps of interpretation and extrapolations back in time. His conclusions in his report on Spruce Tree House provide a good example:

Jesse Walter Fewkes, the first professional archaeologist to work in Mesa Verde, conducted repair and excavation in Cliff Palace along with many other sites during his fourteen years of work on the mesa.

OPPOSITE: *Cliff Palace today*

From the preceding facts it is evident that the people who once inhabited Spruce-tree House were not highly developed in culture, although the buildings show an advanced order of architecture for aborigines of North America. Architecturally the cliff-dwellings excel pueblos of more recent construction. …

The picture of culture drawn from what we know of the life at Spruce-tree House is practically the same as that of a pueblo like Walpi [a village on First Mesa at Hopi] at the time of its discovery by whites, and until about fifty years ago. The people were farmers, timid, industrious, and superstitious. The women were skillful potters and made fine baskets. The men made cloth of good quality and cultivated corn, beans, and melons.

In the long winters the kivas served as the lounging places for the men who were engaged in an almost constant round of ceremonies of dramatic character, which took the place of the pleasures of the chase. They never ventured far from home and rarely met strangers. They had all those unsocial characteristics which an isolated life fosters.

What language they spoke, and whether various Mesa Verde Houses had the same language, at present no one can tell. The culture was selfcentered and apparently well developed. It is not known whether it originated in the Mesa Verde canyons or was completely evolved when it reached there.

Although we know little about the culture of the prehistoric inhabitants of Mesa Verde, it does not follow that we can not find out more. There are many ruins awaiting exploration in this region and future work will reveal much which has been so long hidden.

The pressure of outside tribes, or what may be called human environment, probably had much to do originally with the choice of caves for houses, and the magnificent caverns of the Mesa Verde naturally attracted men as favorable sites for their houses. The habit of huddling together in a limited space, necessitated by a life in the cliffs, possibly developed the composite form which still persists in the pueblo form of architecture.

FORWARDED AUG 12 1907 TO CHIEF CLERK. DEP'T OF THE INTERIOR.

DIVISION OF MAILS & FILES

ALL CORRESPONDENCE SHOULD BE ADDRESSED TO THE SECRETARY

SMITHSONIAN INSTITUTION.
Washington, U.S.A.

UNITED STATES NATIONAL MUSEUM
INTERNATIONAL EXCHANGES
BUREAU OF AMERICAN ETHNOLOGY
NATIONAL ZOOLOGICAL PARK
ASTROPHYSICAL OBSERVATORY

August 12, 1907.

S i r:

I have the honor to acknowledge the receipt of your communication of July 31, inquiring whether it will be practicable to permit Dr. J. Walter Fewkes, of the Bureau of American Ethnology, to take charge of the work of excavation, preservation and repair of the cliff dwellings and other prehistoric ruins in the Mesa Verde National Park, Colorado, for which purpose you state that the sum of $3,000 has been set apart by the Department. In reply I beg to say that the Institution will take pleasure in assigning Dr. Fewkes to this work, but that in view of the recent conference between the officials of the Department and Mr. W. H. Holmes, Chief of the Bureau, and Dr. Fewkes, it is thought advisable to have the latter postpone taking the field until the latter part of the fiscal year - possibly early in April next.

If this suggestion is acceptable to the Department, I may say that it is my belief that an allotment of $2,000 will

desire, but it is presumed that the Institution will be permitted to publish the scientific results of such researches as Dr. Fewkes may be able to make in the course of his operations in the Park.

Assuring you that the action of the Department in offering to place the work of preserving these important

Fewkes was on "loan" from the Smithsonian Institution to complete his work in several Mesa Verde sites.

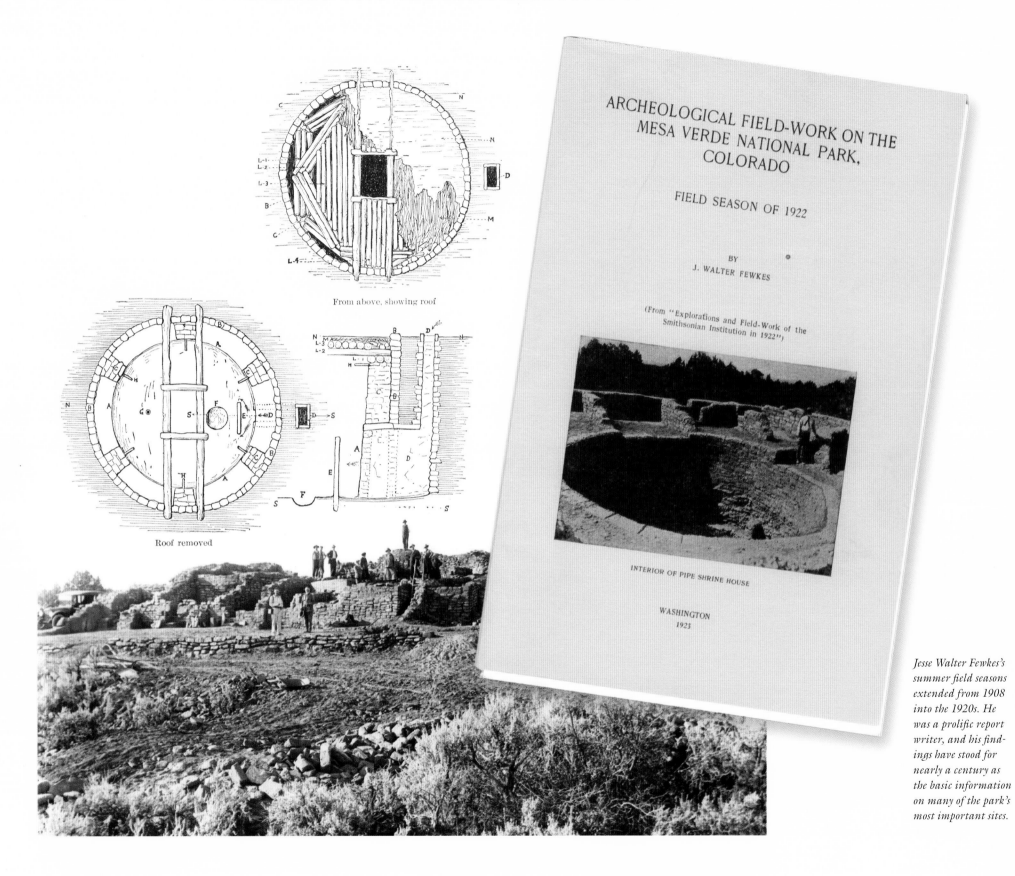

From above, showing roof

Roof removed

ARCHEOLOGICAL FIELD-WORK ON THE
MESA VERDE NATIONAL PARK,
COLORADO

FIELD SEASON OF 1922

BY

J. WALTER FEWKES

(From "Explorations and Field-Work of the
Smithsonian Institution in 1922")

INTERIOR OF PIPE SHRINE HOUSE

WASHINGTON
1923

Jesse Walter Fewkes's summer field seasons extended from 1908 into the 1920s. He was a prolific report writer, and his findings have stood for nearly a century as the basic information on many of the park's most important sites.

Fewkes, fifth from left, sits with his wife and visitors at a campfire circle at Mesa Verde in 1915. His evening campfire talks were the beginning of what has become a grand national park tradition.

ARCHAEOLOGIST-SUPERINTENDENT: JESSE NUSBAUM

Just as Fewkes was beginning his work in the new park, Edgar Hewett brought to Mesa Verde two young up-and-coming archaeologists—Alfred Vincent Kidder and Jesse Nusbaum. Kidder went on to build an illustrious career in Southwest archaeology, while Nusbaum, a talented photographer and builder from Greeley, Colorado, became one of the most significant personalities in the history of Mesa Verde National Park.

Among Jesse Nusbaum's first archaeological jobs in Mesa Verde was cleaning up debris and stabilizing walls in Balcony House. In the fall of 1910, he and a crew—including a stone mason; an engineer; and his father, a building contractor—worked there for ten weeks, repairing cracks and reinforcing the walls. In 1921, Nusbaum was appointed superintendent. During his superintendency, Nusbaum's contributions to Mesa Verde National Park can hardly be overstated. Working with meager funds doled out by a tightfisted Congress, he pursued archaeological projects in the park as he could. He trained a crew in the alcove of Spruce Tree House in the winter of 1924, then moved on to Wetherill Mesa, conducting fieldwork in several sites during the snowy, cold winters of 1924 to 1929.

Jesse Nusbaum, right, and Alfred Vincent Kidder, second from right, came to Mesa Verde in 1908. Both, fresh from Harvard, began their careers here. Nusbaum went on to become one of the park's most influential superintendents.

At times Jesse Nusbaum employed "radical" techniques such as metal reinforcement of walls, as seen here in his 1910 work in Balcony House.

ANALYZING TREE RINGS: A. E. DOUGLASS AND THE NATIONAL GEOGRAPHIC EXPEDITION

In 1923, the First National Geographic Beam Expedition, directed by scientist A. E. Douglass, visited Mesa Verde. Douglass was pioneering a new discipline—dendrochronology—the science of tree-ring dating. By "reading" the annual growth rings in cores of wood, Douglass assembled a master chronology for Southwest archaeology. With cores from wood beams in Mesa Verde structures, he produced dates for the major cliff dwellings, indicating Cliff Palace was built in A.D. 1073, Balcony House from A.D. 1190 until 1206, and Spruce Tree House, one of the latest, from A.D. 1216 until 1262. The tree rings also showed that a prolonged drought gripped the region from A.D. 1276 until 1299. This finding has been invoked for many years as a cause of the final departure of the Pueblo people from the Four Corners.

USING HIS "SIXTH SENSE": JAMES A. LANCASTER

By the early 1930s, the deteriorating condition of the park's major archaeological sites, both cliff dwellings and open pueblos on the mesa tops, was reaching a critical stage. Natural weathering processes, especially water damage, along with the effects of many visitors' footsteps, were taking a heavy toll. A significant program of stabilization and repair, along with surveying, mapping, and photography, was initiated in 1934. Another Edgar Hewett student, Earl Morris, was hired to supervise the work in Cliff Palace, Spruce Tree House, Balcony House, Far View, and others. Morris's choice for crew foreman was James A. Lancaster.

"Al" Lancaster, as everyone knew him, was a pinto bean farmer from near Cortez, Colorado, and son of an Oklahoma homesteader. His first archaeological work was at Lowry Pueblo not far from Cortez. Then he signed on with J. O. Brew at Alkali Ridge, and was also part of the crew at Awatovi on the Hopi Mesas.

Self-taught in archaeology, Al Lancaster seemed to possess a "sixth sense" about where to look for sites. He is widely praised as the one of the best "dirt" archaeologists in the Southwest. According to Robert Lister, who worked with Lancaster, his quick grasp of excavation procedures was "coupled to a farmer's knowledge of the weather, landscape, soils and rocks, dirt moving, carpentry,

Members of the National Geographic Beam Expedition took wood samples from Mesa Verde sites, launching a valuable field of study that fostered accurate dating of Southwest archaeological sites.

stone masonry, practical engineering, and how to get along with Indians and college professors." Despite his deep experience in Southwest archaeology, Lancaster was unassuming about his knowledge. When asked by his biographer, Jenny Adams, whether he liked excavation or stabilization better, Lancaster replied simply, "I loved it all."

Al Lancaster worked for the park service in Mesa Verde over the course of thirty years, from 1934 until 1965, and for another decade beyond that with the Mesa Verde field school. As park managers struggled to protect fragile sites against the onslaught of visitors, archaeologists continued their work in Mesa Verde. Through the 1950s, Al Lancaster led the excavation of sites along Ruins Road (now the Mesa Top Loop Drive), revealing classic early pit houses and displaying for visitors a nearly complete record of habitation at Mesa Verde.

Robert Lister directed the Archaeological Research Center at Mesa Verde, providing college students with field experience and adding data on several park sites.

IN THE FIELD: ROBERT LISTER

In the 1960s, a well-respected field archaeologist from the University of Colorado, Robert Lister, began a decade of fieldwork at Mesa Verde. He and his wife, Florence, combined their archaeological findings in a number of books about Mesa Verde and surrounding Ancestral Puebloan sites, among them *Mesa Verde National Park: Preserving the Past* and *Those Who Came Before: Southwestern Archeology in the National Park System*.

During his five decades studying and writing about the Ancestral Puebloans, Lister spent a great deal of time on Colorado's Western Slope, often with students from the University of Colorado, where he established the archaeology program, and the University of New Mexico, where he taught in the 1970s. Florence Lister describes those years in the field:

> Each year our family would meet the students, who usually numbered about twenty to twenty-five, at the Boulder campus and then convoy them through South Park, over Wolf Creek Pass, down to Durango, and on to Mesa Verde. The field school quarters consisted of a former schoolhouse, whose one classroom served as a dining room and study hall, and an adjacent bunkhouse. There were electricity, hot water, refrigeration—near luxury for a field situation. Our family had two bedrooms and a bath in what was considered to be the teacher's apartment. …
>
> During the program's weeklong tours, we regularly took [the students] through other ruins and contemporary Pueblos in the northern Southwest. It took a great deal of planning and iron will to travel all day, arrive at some chosen stopping place, set up camp and kitchen, and get a hot meal served before general mutiny had erupted.

Continuing his work at Chaco Canyon, Bob Lister joined with the National Park Service staff in the early 1970s as director and chief archaeologist of the Chaco

Canyon archaeological research program. A native New Mexican who never strayed far from the Southwest, he and Florence settled below Mesa Verde in 1988, retiring to Mancos, Colorado. Robert Lister died in May 1990 while visiting an Ancestral Puebloan site.

TAKING A CLOSER LOOK: THE WETHERILL MESA ARCHAEOLOGICAL PROJECT

Archaeological research received a substantial boost in 1958 with the launch of the extensive Wetherill Mesa Archaeological Project. This ambitious, multidisciplinary, million-dollar-plus project was well financed with assistance from the National Geographic Society. After the two-year preliminary survey, more than 800 sites had been found on the mesa west of Chapin. Along with excavations of Long House, Mug House, Step House, and other sites, as well as extensive laboratory work, Wetherill Mesa yielded much finer detail about Mesa Verde's prehistory.

Douglas Osborne supervised the Wetherill Mesa Archaeological Project, and he wrote a lengthy article about it for the February 1964 issue of *National Geographic* magazine:

> For five years now we have dug and studied. In one of the most thorough explorations of the past ever undertaken in this country, we have peered through the lenses of some 28 different sciences to learn the ways of the prehistoric cliff dwellers of Mesa Verde. …
>
> By studying fecal matter 700 years old, we have learned a great deal about [the cliff dwellers'] diet, nutrition, and parasitic diseases.
>
> Tree rings in the beams of their cliff-hanging homes not only enable us to date the ruins, but by comparison with growth rings in trees of today we can get a good idea of their weather.
>
> From centuries-old pollen we have found what plants grew here in those days—and gained evidence pointing to hitherto-unknown crops in the ancient Indian community.
>
> Cores that give us cross sections of soil combined with the pollen studies tell a sad story of changing conditions—of growing erosion, ruined farmland, possibly a prehistoric dust bowl.
>
> We can even ache with these vanished people, for their bones show ravages of arthritis as well as decayed and throbbing teeth.
>
> Yet the story ends on a happier note, for among the Indians of today in the sunny pueblos far to the south, almost identical artifacts show that many of the ways, if not the blood, of the cliff dwellers survive to this day. …
>
> Wetherill Mesa, found in 1890, is named for the pioneer family that fathered Mesa Verde archaeology. The early explorers and archaeologists they guided combed the area, and of course entered and stripped most of the cliff dwellings of any artifacts left above ground. But they did not find all the caches that were made and forgotten a thousand years ago.
>
> Our painstaking survey located many untouched ruins and caches. Archaeologist Alden C. Hayes, working alone, found the first of them. He entered a small ruin in upper Rock Canyon by climbing a log propped against the cliff.

The Wetherill Mesa project was funded in part by the National Geographic Society, and its results appeared in an in-depth article in the society's magazine in 1964.

Douglas Osborne surveys the incredible collection of fine Mesa Verde ceramics collected during the Wetherill Mesa Archaeological Project.

After the fieldwork on Wetherill Mesa came many long hours of laboratory time involving a talented interdisciplinary team.

CLOCKWISE, FROM TOP, *Wetherill Laboratory in full operation, March 1965;* archaeologist Alden C. Hayes; project personnel *examining a* National Geographic *article on Mesa Verde;* R. P. Wheeler *and Lucy Wheeler labeling pottery; Gretchen Hayes recording collected data.*

After recording the site, he started down, hesitated a moment, went back and peered into a crevice at the back of the cave. He found a bundle of digging sticks—sharpened hardwood staffs used to till the soil—and a large black-on-white painted olla, a jar used to store precious water from spring rains for the dry days of summer.

Al still does not know why he went back to stare into that particular crack. He couldn't get the pot out alone, so he returned the next day, Saturday, his day off, with his son Eric. He had to get that pot out intact—and he did. It had been there, unharmed, for 700 years. ...

Grandest of all is Long House, second largest cliff dwelling in the park (after Cliff Palace on Chapin Mesa). Long House grips you. I have heard many a man gasp as I led him to the cliff edge above the ruin.

George S. Cattanach and Art Rohn started digging in Long House in the spring of 1959—the first time a full-scale dig had been attempted there. Just clearing away the rubble was a tremendous job. ...

One aspect of Long House offers a problem of magnitude. If we could answer it, I feel, we would be very close indeed to some of the answers to the key mysteries of Mesa Verde.

The question: Why is the ratio of kivas to rooms so great? Kivas were used as we use our churches, as religious and social centers. Long House had 22 kivas, plus a great kiva, to some 150 rooms—one kiva to seven rooms. This is almost double the ratio in most other cliff dwellings.

This situation suggests that the people from several of the smaller surface houses crowded into the great cliff dwelling. Each incoming group or religious society had to have its own kiva.

Does this mean that those who lived in Long House were priest-ridden and spent an uneconomic amount of time in religious activity? Perhaps. Does it mean that there was an increasing tension as people in cramped quarters eyed the space taken up by the numerous kivas? Maybe. Perhaps the people were turning, ever hopefully, finally frantically, to their gods as they battled whatever it was that was driving them from their homes. ...

We did far more than dig on Wetherill Mesa; we preserved. These ruins are fragile and their numbers limited. If Mesa Verde was to continue to be one of the great outdoor

museums of the world, we had to prepare these remnants of the past to survive long into the future.

So we strengthened the ancient structures, shoring up and bracing the enfeebled walls, providing firm foundations and protection from the elements. We did not attempt to rebuild; that would have been false. Instead, we treated the ruins as a restorer would an old painting, carefully giving them a new lease on life.

Someday a few years from now Wetherill Mesa will have good roads and trails. ... Then you will be able to come into this splendid frame of cliff and canyon, and see the mysterious past with your own eyes.

Your first impression, as mine has often been on first entering these dwellings of a forgotten people, may be: "This is impossible. These walls, these pots, these discarded corn husks, and roofs still blackened by cooking fires—these things cannot be 700 years old."

But they can be. They are.

A NEW POINT OF VIEW: LARRY NORDBY

Water damage to Cliff Palace, unarguably Mesa Verde's most famous cliff dwelling, prompted emergency work in the site beginning in 1995. Park archaeologists Larry Nordby and Joel Brisbin began meticulous architectural documentation of the entire dwelling. Their revised interpretations were the first major new ideas about Cliff Palace since Jesse Walter Fewkes excavated the dwelling in 1909.

Advances in computers have played a large part in the development of new archaeological studies at Mesa Verde, as has the evolution of archaeology over the last century. When J. W. Fewkes excavated, he had simple objectives in a world that had not yet discovered the Southwest nor experienced the relatively new idea of national parks. He wanted to publicize the parks and interest people, so he excavated major sites and made them safe for people to visit. Archaeological work in the past century has resulted

OPPOSITE: *Exciting new work in Cliff Palace was reported to the public in a 1999 issue of* Smithsonian *magazine. The computer-generated floor plan of Cliff Palace resulted in new interpretations of this dwelling.*

42

in a better understanding of archaeology as a link between modern people and ancestral places and has taught us that objects and buildings can tell a story, as opposed to just serving as curiosities in museums.

Archaeologists now collect tightly focused observations based on carefully designed research objectives. They use computers to handle this information, as digital images, such that very precise three-dimensional models can be created. They also use computers to handle hundreds of data fields for each room and are better able to understand connections between such diverse kinds of information as room size, doorway design, decorative wall paintings, and tree-ring dates. This in turn helps identify and explain past construction behaviors and social relationships.

In their study of Cliff Palace, Nordby and Brisbin's analysis changed the definition of what a room was and thereby, the total number of rooms at the site. Rather than 220 rooms, as previously tallied, Cliff Palace contains only 150 "enclosed spaces." Further, only about twenty-five of the rooms were actually lived in; the other 125 or so were storerooms, grinding rooms, or communal spaces. Thus, Nordby estimated that only about a hundred people actually lived in Cliff Palace. He also observed mirror symmetry to the rooms and a wall that divided the dwelling into two parts.

Author David Roberts went with Larry Nordby into

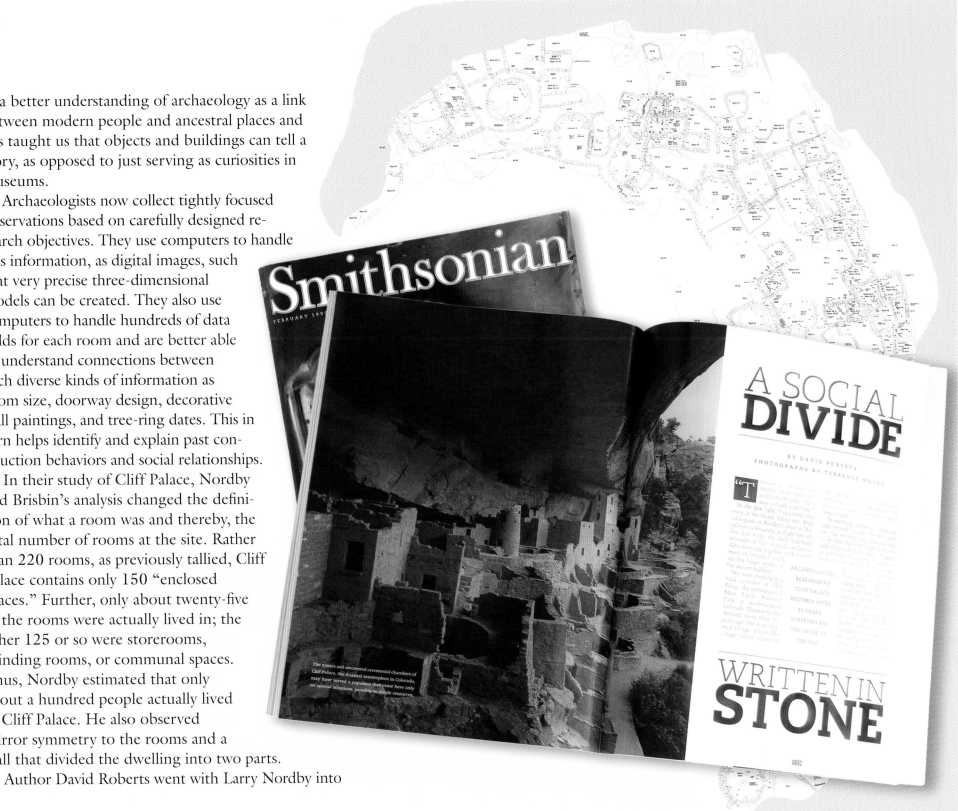

Cliff Palace and wrote of the visit in a feature article that appeared in the February 1999 issue of *Smithsonian* magazine.

"There's no reason for them to build that wall," said Larry Nordby. "All it does is block your way. ... Something dramatic happened right around A.D. 1280," Nordby went on. "Let me show you what you had to do after that date to get from one side of this wall to the other." Tagging at his heels, I followed the archaeologist as he strolled from passageway to plaza, his right hand regularly tapping a zigzag series of partitions cunningly built into contiguous rooms uninterrupted by door or windows. "To do it, you have to come clear outside. ..."

"The wall splits Cliff Palace," Nordby concluded. "It divides the place into completely separate parts. ..."

What, then, did the symmetries and the dividing wall suggest was going on in Cliff Palace around 1280? ...

[Nordby] ... had begun to wonder whether he was detecting the architectural footprints of a social division along the lines of what anthropologists call moieties—twinned affiliations at a larger level than clan or kinship, which helped organize a society and define each member's role within it. ...

"With all the stress the people are exposed to by 1280," Nordby ventured, "that's when things start to get tough. That's when social dislocations start to happen. I imagine that Cliff Palace, with its small caretaker population, was some kind of redistribution center of goods—maybe surplus corn—for a larger population that came to receive it. For the first time, there's a new pressure for someone to take charge: you can't just have 300 people in a room all shouting out what they want.

"I imagine the dual division of Cliff Palace around 1280 was an attempt to manage that stress."

THE WRITING ON THE WALL: FRED BLACKBURN

In a special project for Mesa Verde, Four Corners archaeologist Fred Blackburn searched from 1998 through 2001 for historical inscriptions in six cliff dwellings in the park: Balcony House, Cliff Palace, Spruce Tree House, Hemenway House, Little Hemenway House, and Honeymoon House. Half the alcove sites were easily accessible, while the others were reached by climbing trees and following old hand- and toehold trails. Honeymoon House, named by Blackburn and his coworkers, was so little known that it contained only one inscription.

In each dwelling, a systematic room-by-room survey was done. Each inscription was mapped and drawn. In all, 2,200 separate inscriptions were documented, revealing many of the first entries made by explorers, photographers, guides, visitors, park personnel, and other non-Indians into the sites between 1880 and the early 1900s. This early "graffiti" provides an important primary resource, creating what Blackburn calls an "expeditionary history" of the park. The inscriptions—names, dates, room numbers, sometimes complete addresses—were made with charcoal, paint, and stencils, even bullet lead. Particular places seemed to invite people to record their passage, becoming veritable registries of early visitors. Many of the inscriptions were faint; some had been obliterated by intention or by weathering.

The earliest legible dates, from Hemenway and Little Hemenway House, were from between 1880 and 1890. The oldest found in Cliff Palace was a date of 1885. A few inscriptions were of recent vintage—in the kiva in Spruce Tree House open to the public there were dates between 1960 and 1990. Also in Spruce Tree House one poet-to-be, making an attempt at profundity, etched these words: "All Ye that should wander here, be better men your time is near, go think it over."

Beyond documenting history, this kind of sleuthing allows a correlation of artifact collections in museums with archaeological sites. It is a technique called "reverse archaeology" that Blackburn pioneered in Grand Gulch in southeast Utah. One of the more fascinating findings at Mesa Verde involved an 1892 and 1893 collection for the World's Fair in Chicago. Blackburn discussed it in his report on Mesa Verde inscriptions:

ABOVE: *An inscription left by W. H. Hayes sits on a doorway lintel at Hemenway house. Hayes was one of the first settlers of Mancos.*

LEFT: *Fred Blackburn at work in Hemenway House*

One of the goals of this project was to allow us to make a direct connection between museum artifacts and their original locations in rooms in each site; a process called "reverse archaeology." One of these museum collections, the Wilmarth collection of 1892 and 1893, is curated at the Colorado State Historical Society. The collection was made for the Colorado State exhibit at the 1893 World's Fair in Chicago. At that time A. T. Wilmarth was the chief of the Colorado State Historical Department of the World's Fair. There are 70 artifacts in the collection. Thirty-three are from Balcony House, 29 are from Cliff Palace, and eight are from Spruce Tree House.

During our fieldwork, we think that we located some room numbers written by Arthur T. Wilmarth and his expedition in Balcony House, Cliff Palace, and Spruce Tree House. We do not have a standard archaeological report of the Wilmarth Expedition so there is only the museum inventory record of the link between the assigned room numbers and the artifacts. We are sure of each artifact's association with each site. We have taken the list of room numbers presently used and compared the room numbers found written in the rooms to suggest the 1892–1893 location of the artifacts. Care must be taken not to assume too much without

further evidence. We hope future research will provide connections between other room numbers and the artifacts. …

With the information on room numbers … we were able to trace 18 artifacts from Cliff Palace to the room, general room area, or kiva in which they were found. …

MAINTAINING THE SITES: THE STABILIZATION CREW

One of the first questions that occurs to Mesa Verde visitors is whether the stonework in the dwellings is original. Some is, and some is not. Stabilizing the 800-year-old sites—to mitigate or prevent deterioration from weathering and other causes—has been an active pursuit in the park ever since Jesse Walter Fewkes worked at Mesa Verde in the early twentieth century. In the 1930s, systematic stabilization efforts began, and with varying degrees of success park staff have striven to duplicate the original masonry. Crews still work both at "front country" and "backcountry" sites, re-pointing mortar joints, weeding, and sweeping. Occasionally they have to reach remote places by helicopter and erect ladders or rappel into the sites.

Through the years, the stabilization crew members were mostly Navajo, and they still are. Among the first was Sam Yellowhorse, who brought in Raymond Begay and others who knew each other from participating in Navajo *Yeibichai* dances. Al Lancaster put them to work.

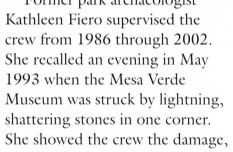

Stabilization crew in Balcony House. Back Row (standing): Gene Trujillo, Willie Begay, Kee John, Raymond Begay Front row (kneeling): Kathy Fiero; Arnold John

Former park archaeologist Kathleen Fiero supervised the crew from 1986 through 2002. She recalled an evening in May 1993 when the Mesa Verde Museum was struck by lightning, shattering stones in one corner. She showed the crew the damage, but they were obviously troubled by something. Fiero realized that lightning required special attention, and before Navajos would reenter a building it had to be cleansed. A medicine man was brought in and the proper ceremony was held.

In an article entitled "Room Service" in *Plateau Journal*, Fiero wrote about how the crew works and the cultural awakening she personally experienced through the years with them:

> Dirt (*slish*), water (*to*), stone (*tse*)—it is amazing what can be produced from such basic materials. These are what the ancestors of the Pueblo Indians used to build Balcony House, Cliff Palace, and other extraordinary structures in the Southwest, and they are what we use today to maintain them. As early as the 1920s Portland cement was used on the ruins for wall caps, and later, in the 50s and 60s, for wall repairs. But through the years it became obvious that hard Portland could damage softer stone. The stones crack and deteriorate before the hard cement mortar does, when it should be the other way around: mortar should be the sacrificial material, the one that erodes first. So now we use plain dirt mortar just as the people who built these places did; or we use a dirt mortar amended with acrylic polymer that still is softer than the surrounding stones. ...
>
> Together with a crew hired more for their dancing than masonry skills, I work on remnants—remnants of the past, the past of the ancestors of the Pueblo Indians. Anasazi, we call them, though it's not the choice of Pueblo people. It's a Navajo term and continues to be used by our now multi-ethnic but predominantly Navajo crew. Perhaps we ourselves are remnants—of a past with a much smaller park staff, few rules and regulations.
>
> The crew is respectful of fragments of the past. Once while working at Balcony House to improve drainage in the site, a Navajo crewman found a small covered pot that he felt had ceremonial importance to the Anasazi. He reburied the pot in a location that would not be disturbed during the project. More than ten years later, just before he retired, he dug it up and gave it to the crew chief. It is now in the Mesa Verde collections.
>
> Some people bring up the question of authenticity and may think the new should stand apart from the remnants of the old, so as not to confuse the two, but we're respectful of the vestiges of early technique.
>
> "Don't make a nice wall," Al Lancaster used to say, according to Raymond. He wanted the new work to look Anasazi.
>
> One day Raymond and I were near the top of a steep trail. It was hot and we had spent a hard day working in the backcountry. We were catching our breath leaning on a boulder in the shade of a tree. Suddenly Raymond got out his Leatherman, stepped across the trail, and cut and removed an old length of wire strangling a juniper tree.
>
> The old and the new. They both have a place.

NATIVE AMERICAN GRAVES PROTECTION AND REPATRIATION ACT (NAGPRA)

The Native American Graves Protection and Repatriation Act, passed in 1990, requires all federal museums that hold Native American human remains, grave goods, and sacred objects to develop plans to repatriate this material to culturally affiliated tribes.

To comply with the law, Mesa Verde National Park's curatorial staff spent five years completing an inventory of all such items. The inventory showed that the park's museum collection contains the human remains representing the physical remains of at least 1,524 individuals and 4,863 associated funerary objects. The remains came primarily from the 1960s Wetherill Mesa Archaeological Project.

The park also completed a non-invasive physical anthropological assessment of the human remains to document evidence of disease, trauma, age, sex, and size. At the same time, a cultural affiliation study was undertaken by anthropologists at Fort Lewis College to determine which contemporary Native American tribes are culturally affiliated to the Ancestral Puebloan remains in the park. Twenty-four tribes were identified: the Hopi Tribe, Pueblo of Acoma, Pueblo of Cochiti, Pueblo of Isleta, Pueblo of Laguna, Pueblo of Jemez, Pueblo of Nambe, Pueblo of Sandia, Pueblo of San Felipe, Navajo Nation, Picuris Pueblo, Pueblo of Pojoaque, Pueblo of San Ildefonso, Pueblo of San Juan, Pueblo of Santo Domingo, Santa Clara Pueblo, Santa Ana Pueblo, Southern Ute Tribe, Taos Pueblo, Ute Mountain Ute Tribe, Pueblo of Zia, Ysleta del Sur Pueblo, Pueblo of Zuni, and Tesuque Pueblo.

Park staff have been consulting with these tribes since 1993. The tribes requested that the human remains and grave goods be reburied in the park when repatriation is

Douglas Osborne and Florence Ellis consulted with members of the Taos Pueblo for the Wetherill Mesa project.

accomplished. The park announced the completion of its NAGPRA inventory in August 1999 and designated the Pueblos of Acoma, Zia, and Zuni and the Hopi Tribe as the official repatriating tribes, with the tribes' agreement.

Together the park and tribes have worked to organize all of the human remains with their grave goods and find a suitable location for reburial, which will be accomplished pending the outcome of a dispute regarding the park's cultural affiliation determinations.

During the park's consultation meetings, many other areas of park management have been discussed. The first and foremost event was the identification by tribal representatives of sacred material and grave goods that were on display in the park's museum and at the visitor center. These materials were removed. The tribal representatives have also worked with the park staff on updating interpretive material to more accurately reflect the tribes' oral history regarding the use of their ancestral sites at Mesa Verde National Park.

The positive long-term result of the NAGPRA Act is the ongoing dialogue that National Park staff and tribal members enjoy. Representatives from the 24 tribes engage in discussion with park managers on a variety of topics from post-fire effects and invasive weed management, to consultation on research programs and site stabilization.

CHAPTER 4

DEVELOPING A NATIONAL PARK: TRANSPORTATION, LODGING, AND AMENITIES

Without question, southwestern Colorado is an isolated land. Initially, it took weeks to reach it from Denver or Santa Fe, and early travelers found it hard going, even monotonous. This country had little to attract settlers or visitors until gold and silver were found in the nearby San Juan Mountains. Then came the rush.

Eventually, that nineteenth-century wonder, the railroad, chugged into view, and it suddenly became easy, safe, and fast to travel into the region. Henry David Thoreau, who did not particularly like railroads, commented, "We do not ride on the railroad; it rides upon us." He was right: the railroad forever changed southwestern Colorado.

Once people could easily get to the park, new needs had to be met: a comfortable bed, a hot meal, a sheltered place to learn about and enjoy Mesa Verde. Park managers, concessionaires, and the Civilian Conservation Corps quickly stepped in, obtaining funding, building structures, and supplying the services a visiting public required.

TRANSPORTATION

Railroads promoted Mesa Verde and brought visitors in leisure and at a speed that was unimaginable a generation before. Then came the automobile and the airplane,

and Mesa Verde National Park became an easily attainable destination point.

Early visitors could take the train to a depot near the foot of the mesa, but had to disembark and go by horse or carriage up its sheer face. In 1913, the first horse and wagon arrived at Spruce Tree House from Mancos. A year later the road into the park was pronounced suitable for automobile traffic, and a gaggle of cars caravanned in to prove it could be done. In 1915, ex-ranger Charles B. Kelly was granted the "auto livery" concession. The excursion was not cheap—it cost $25 for two people. Still, a park pamphlet published that year advised that "The trip over the Government road should be taken only by parties who are experienced in the handling and controlling

OPPOSITE: Lookout Point stands as a distinctive Mesa Verde landmark.

The rugged landscape of Lookout Point has not changed over the past century.

49

Mesa Verde's remoteness adds to its allure, but travel up onto the mesa in the early days was a challenge. Decals were used to promote visitor safety.

LEFT: *Call box on entrance road;* RIGHT: *Unstable shale made roads challenging.*

In 1916, the road through the Rocky Mountains over Wolf Creek Pass and into Durango was complete. Though it was a frightening single-lane route at first, its existence marked a major step toward opening western Colorado to easterners. The gospel of the "good roads" movement was sung loud and long, and the results showed in visitation figures at Mesa Verde. Each year visitation increased steadily, from about 660 people in 1915 to 2,800 in 1920 to 16,800 in 1928. Train travel was already starting to decline by the late 1920s, outrun by the autonomy of the automobile.

of horses and should not be attempted in seasons when rainfall in quantity occurs." The steep grade in the Point Lookout section of the road was especially subject to washouts.

Telephone call boxes were installed along the road. At the bottom of the hill, a sign ordered drivers to "Stop: All persons are forbidden passing this point without first calling the Superintendent's office, Phone No. 11." A like sign was posted at the top of the hill, so whoever called first was given the go-ahead to proceed up or down the road. If someone was already headed up, then the person at the top had to wait, and vice versa.

Mesa Verde made a big impression on early visitors. Among them was Lena Lenton, of Boulder, Colorado, who was ecstatic with her visit on August 16, 1919. She exuded this testimonial, included in a touring company brochure:

> For five years I dreamed of it—in the summer I talked of it—in the winter I drove the household wild by repeating its wonders and my desire to reach the Mesa Verde National

The Knife Edge portion of the old entrance road was well named.

Park—at last I am here and all my dreams are realized. The wonderful trip on the narrow gauge along the winding rivers suspended over mountain peaks and lonely vistas of pine forests would have been satisfactory enough for one summer vacation, but combined with the wonderful drive from Mancos to the Park and culminated with these unique old world ruins, who could ask for anything better? I leave with the determination to spread abroad the fame of the Mesa Verde Park, with its wonderful accommodations of house and board for the weary tourist who sojourns beneath its roof, and its fascinating relics of a bygone people.

T he annual Sociability Run of Oldsmobile Owners from Denver to Mesa Verde was a unique combination of railroad and automobile travel to the park. The club members' automobiles were shipped by the Denver & Rio Grande Railroad from Denver to Mancos, Colorado.

A trip to Mesa Verde—requiring connections by rail, stagecoach, and later automobile—was a huge adventure. The towns of Durango and Mancos in Colorado, or Gallup in New Mexico, were the jumping-off points for those making the journey. The last stretch, the memorable entrance road, finally got them onto the mesa top.

"BUILDING" A NATIONAL PARK

In the 1920s, Superintendent Jesse Nusbaum and his wife, Aileen, designed and built their own house on Chapin Mesa, of local stone in an adapted pueblo architectural style. Nusbaum also oversaw construction of rock and timber structures for park headquarters, a museum, and residences for park employees. Aileen Nusbaum, a nurse, even had a small hospital built. Jesse Nusbaum opened a free public campground and tried to upgrade Oddie Jeep's Spruce Tree Camp accommodations.

Struggling to administer the park with the slim funds allocated by Congress through the 1920s, Nusbaum sought help from outside sources. One promising donor was John D. Rockefeller Jr., whom Nusbaum squired around the park over the Fourth of July weekend in 1924. Nusbaum hoped to convince Rockefeller to contribute toward the completion of a new fireproof museum. The museum had already gotten under way with a donation of several thousand dollars from a San Francisco woman named Mrs. Stella Leviston.

After a rapid chase of the Rockefeller party in their Packards and two other "large cars" entering the park from Mancos, Nusbaum caught up with them. Rockefeller got

into Nusbaum's car and went with him into the park and proceeded on a tour. Three days later, an obviously energized Nusbaum wrote a six-page, single-spaced letter to the director of the National Park Service giving incredible detail about the visit. His original spelling is retained.

Mr. Rockefeller was tremendously pleased with the trip over the north rim, saying that he had never supposed such a road existed from which one could survey so much magnificent country. We proceeded leisurely to the park. …

Mrs. Raynolds and Mrs. Nusbaum has scoured the country for the best of steaks, fruit, vegetables etc. and had prepared a wonderful beef-steak fry for them on the rim of Soda Canyon, just above Balcony House. A ranger was posted to keep the "curious" away should they attempt to see what was going on. While the women prepared the supper, I took the party thru Balcony House and gave them a wonderful view of the ruin in the fading light of day. When we returned, supper was ready, and since they had not eaten since morning, they did ample justice to the fine dinner. We staid about

the camp fire and talked for hours it seems. …

The next day was given over entirely in the morning to the ruins … The afternoon was spent in and about camp in going over buildings, watching the Navaho women weave, visiting the Museum etc., and then a good long visit at our home. … Later, when it was cooler, we took them thru Spruce Tree House. That night I gave a camp fire talk while it was getting dark enough to give the pageant. We then took them to the cliff edge, and reserved the best position for the party. Mrs. Nusbaum went down with the Indians and they went thru their parts in wonderful fashion. He was tremendously pleased, and when Mrs. Nusbaum came up from the canyon with the eighteen Indians, Sam Ahkeah, one of our best, asked for Mr. Rockefeller, and when he had introduced his fellow players, took his turquoise ring from his finger and gave it to Mr. Rockefeller . … Mr. Rockefeller was quite overcome and made a wonderful short talk to the Navajos. So ended the second day.

Jesse Nusbaum, with his wife and stepson, roughed it in the park much as visitors did.

Nusbaum made sure John D. Rockefeller Jr. (left) received a grand tour during his 1924 visit.

Sketch of a park administration building shows Jesse Nusbaum's interest in designing structures compatible with Puebloan architecture.

BELOW: *Nusbaum's residence, now park headquarters, reflected his aesthetics.*

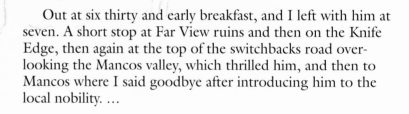

Out at six thirty and early breakfast, and I left with him at seven. A short stop at Far View ruins and then on the Knife Edge, then again at the top of the switchbacks road overlooking the Mancos valley, which thrilled him, and then to Mancos where I said goodbye after introducing him to the local nobility. …

Nusbaum's hospitality was successful: Rockefeller responded with a promise of $2,000 to complete the museum, up to $1,000 for excavations in Spruce Tree House, and more for other possible needs. Nusbaum concludes his letter by expressing how impressed he was by his guest and the pleasure he felt from his generosity. "Mesa Verde now has a most rosy future ahead, the extent of which will depend on us."

From 1941 until 1945, the years of World War II, park visitation plummeted, CCC camps closed, budget and staff were cut, and hard-hit ranchers pressed again to graze cattle in the park, a battle Jesse Nusbaum had already fought and won once. During the war years, however, Nusbaum succeeded in helping craft a solution to the park's long-standing problem of water supply. Water of good quality and sufficient quantity was a major drawback for the park,

DERIC IN MESA VERDE

Jesse Nusbaum's stepson, Deric, showed many of the same interests as his stepfather. When Deric was only eleven years old, he was part of the crew that his father trained in Spruce Tree House in the 1920s. Deric helped with the excavations of that decade and returned to Mesa Verde again in 1947 and 1948 as a full-fledged archaeologist with the Gila Pueblo Foundation. They excavated an early pit house at what is known as the Twin Trees site, work that visitors along the Mesa Top Loop Drive can still see.

At the tender age of twelve, with the help of his mother, Deric wrote a book. *Deric in Mesa Verde* was published in 1926 by G. P. Putnam's Sons, part of its series Boys Writing for Boys. Young Deric describes his years growing up in the park—snowshoeing in the woods in winter, riding horseback to visit Navajos, working alongside excavation crews in the park's archaeological sites—a life of nearly continuous excitement and adventure that would have been the dream and envy of every child, boy and girl alike, in the country. In the first chapter Deric wrote:

Most of the time in the summer I go arrowhead hunting, or on hikes to out-of-the-way ruins, or just through the woods. I have learned to walk without making any noise like the Indian hunters do (of course I don't shoot anything, this Park is a game preserve) but I do this because if the little wild animals are not frightened, I can get up quite close to them. There are lots of rabbits, chipmunks, squirrels, weasels, bobcats, porcupines and many others. ...

The mountain lions come in fairly close to Camp after the snow falls in winter, and the coyotes come right into our backyard. ...

Beginning in early spring, my hikes sometimes lead me to places where wild flowers bloom. I am helping mother get a collection of them for the Museum. ...

I thought that it was pretty dry at first, but after I got on to it I liked it.

Sometimes I take horseback trips. We have a dandy horse named Rube, that I like to ride. ...

Our roads are usually closed with snow in November and aren't opened until April. It's heaps of fun to be "snowed in." Twice a month a ranger takes a horse and an extra pack horse, and goes over the thirty mile trail to the south, to Mancos for the mail and fresh meat.

It's hard to tell which I like best up here, summer or winter. Of course I can get around more in summer, but in winter I showshoe, ski and coast. I go for an hour before lessons in the morning and most of the afternoon. ...

Best of all after the season closes, Dad has time to take me to some of the unexcavated ruins and we do some exploring. As I am planning to be an archaeologist, this interests me very much. It beats "Treasure Island."

In the frontispiece for Deric in Mesa Verde, *the young author peers out of a Mesa Verde doorway.*

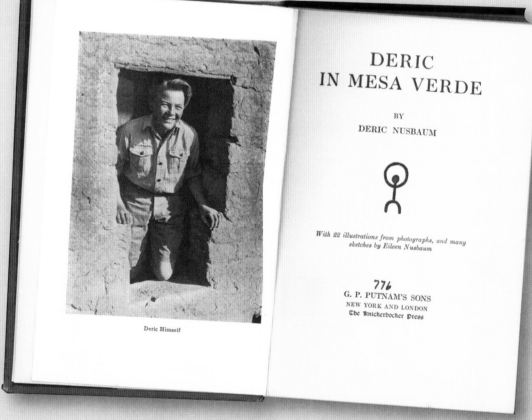

Deric Himself

DERIC
IN MESA VERDE

BY
DERIC NUSBAUM

With 22 illustrations from photographs, and many sketches by Eileen Nusbaum

776
G. P. PUTNAM'S SONS
NEW YORK AND LONDON
The Knickerbocker Press

Spruce Tree Camp, as it looked around 1908, was the main facility for visitor accommodations.

56

and had been since the earliest days. Through the 1940s, the Mancos area benefited from federal funds for irrigation projects. One project included a pipeline from the West Mancos River up to the park, assuring for the first time plentiful good water for Mesa Verde. Just before the pipeline was finished in 1951, Jesse Nusbaum retired from the park service, ending an illustrious career.

THE FIRST PARK CONCESSIONS

In 1911, Wesley Martin was hired as temporary ranger, and with his wife, Emma, received the first concessions permit "to furnish meals and sleeping quarters" at Spruce Tree Camp. Emma could charge seventy-five cents for meals and fifty cents for "sleeping quarters," that is, a bed in a tent. The Martins stayed a year.

In 1915, the camping concession was won by Mrs. Oddie Jeep, daughter of park superintendent Thomas Rickner and wife of ranger Fred Jeep. She held the permit until 1929. First reports were less than lustrous about the facilities at Spruce Tree Camp: crude, minimally furnished accommodations, poor meals, and littered grounds. But things began to look up, so much so that in 1918 Spruce Tree Camp won high marks from government inspectors:

> The service is first class in every respect, exceptional in fact, when the difficulties of transportation are considered. The sleeping accommodations are clean and comfortable. The bedrooms are all located in tents 9 by 12 feet with board side walls up about four feet and board floors, with rugs placed near beds. Clear cold spring water is supplied in each tent for bathing purposes. Pitchers and glasses are provided so that guests may obtain hot water from the main hotel building if desired. The dining room is in the main building, in which is located the office and registration facilities. The camp is in direct telephone connection with the

Lodging varied from canvas-sided tent cabins to the real thing with more-luxurious amenities.

railroad and the Superintendent's office in Mancos.

The meals served at this camp are worthy of special mention. The idea of the general quality of the service may be gained from the fact that fresh cream was served with the fruit and cereals. Fresh fruit was served as well. This is unusual, in a dry country so removed from rail transportation. The employees at the camp and throughout the park were competent and very courteous. Such little services as seeing that drinking water was available to returning hikers after visiting the cliff dwellings, etc., indicated a first class conception on the part of the management of what good hotel service is.

Not long after Mrs. Jeep took over the concession, archaeologist Jesse Nusbaum launched regular ranger-guided tours to sites and opened a free public campground on the rim of Spruce Tree Canyon that could accommodate a hundred cars. He also continued the tradition of evening campfire programs and brought in Navajos to perform special dances and songs. In 1922 and 1923, an immense improvement occurred when the park, with state help, rebuilt the scenic Knife Edge entrance road, shortening the distance up to the cliff dwellings by about five miles.

Although Mrs. Jeep continued her Spruce Tree Camp concession, Nusbaum had it moved across the road from the museum and park headquarters. Lodging was expanded and improved, with the addition of more floored tents ($4 dollars a night) and two dozen cottages ($4.50 a night), some with fireplaces. In 1929, the Denver & Rio Grande Railroad's newly founded Mesa Verde Park Company purchased the concession. In 1930, just over 18,000 people visited Mesa Verde, an all-time high.

THE CIVILIAN CONSERVATION CORPS

During the years of the Great Depression, Mesa Verde experienced severe budget cuts, but the park was helped greatly by the work of the Civilian Conservation Corps. The first CCC camp was established in Mesa Verde in 1933 in Prater Canyon, where more than 200 men were housed. Year-round camps soon were built on Chapin Mesa near park headquarters. All of the camps were military in design and operation. The enrollees, unemployed young men mostly eighteen to twenty-three years old,

signed on for six-month stints; twenty-five of the thirty dollars they made each month was sent back home. They worked on roads, trails, and museum dioramas, archaeological excavations, insect and porcupine control, and even as visitor guides. Their especially fine masonry work can still be seen throughout the park. The CCC camps closed in Mesa Verde in 1942.

OPPOSITE: The much-beloved dioramas, still on exhibit in the Chapin Mesa Archaeological Museum, were conceived and built by members of the Civilian Conservation Corps. Details in them show humor and imagination.

The park entrance road, traversing unstable slopes, was perennially under construction or repair. The CCC performed much of the work.

Some CCC enrollees at Mesa Verde distinguished themselves as publishers. Their own Cliff Dweller Press put out a regular newsletter, "The Cliff Dweller," which was typeset and printed on an old Gordon handpress. It was illustrated with original linoleum block prints. Reported in the pages were the comings and goings of CCC enrollees—both locally and at other camps—park happenings, opinion pieces, field notes, and encouraging words from the camp commander.

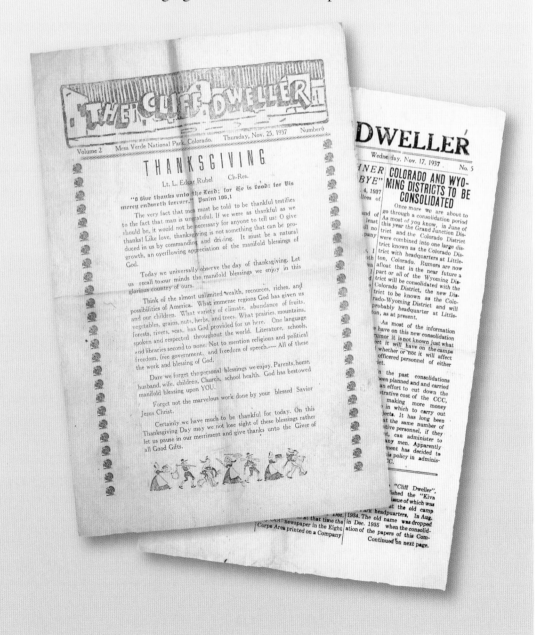

THE MESA VERDE PARK COMPANY

An important event in the park's history transpired in 1937, when Ansel Hall purchased the Mesa Verde Park Company, which had gone bankrupt as a subsidiary of the Denver & Rio Grande Railroad.

Hall, writes historian Duane Smith, was "a rare combination of romantic idealist and practical businessman." A graduate of the University of California's first forestry class, he went on to become chief naturalist for the National Park Service. While he held that post, Hall also organized the ambitious Rainbow Bridge–Monument Valley Expedition, a field training ground for students in the wilds of northeast Arizona. At its conclusion, Hall resigned from the park service and assumed control of concessions in Mesa Verde.

After Ansel Hall's death in 1962, the enterprise passed down to his son, Roger Hall, and then to son-in-law William Winkler, husband of Hall's daughter Merrie. The sale of the Mesa Verde Company in 1976 to the ARA Company ended forty years of the individual private concessionaire in the park and marked a significant shift to large corporate concession operations that are now the norm in many national parks.

Despite conflicts with the park over contracts and rates, Hall held to his belief that visitors deserved quality interpretive experiences while they were in the park. He put his talents toward writing and artwork alongside his business skills.

THE IMPROVEMENTS OF MISSION 66

In 1956, Mesa Verde celebrated its fiftieth anniversary as a national park. That year also saw the launch of Mission 66. This ambitious ten-year initiative throughout the

Far View Lodge, operated by the Mesa Verde Company, was built as part of Mission 66 to upgrade lodging. Meals were served there as well. The lodge and restaurant still operate today and are favorite destinations for many visitors. The Metate Room restaurant is currently ranked one of the top 10 restaurants in Colorado.

FAR LEFT: *Ansel Hall greets flight attendants with Frontier Airlines.*

The Denver Post's Empire Magazine *published a feature on the park in 1963, just as visitation was rising and Mission 66 projects were opening to accommodate more people.*

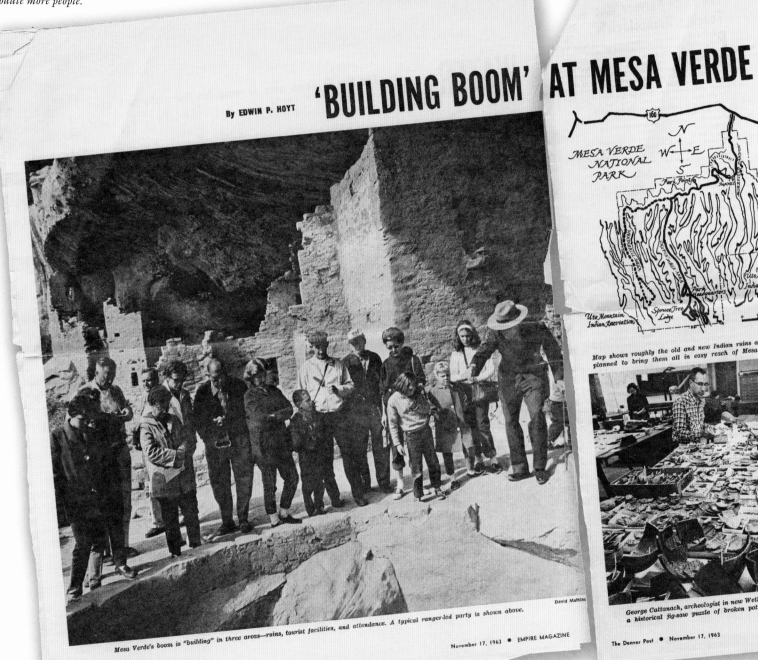

By EDWIN P. HOYT

'BUILDING BOOM' AT MESA VERDE

Mesa Verde's boom is "building" in three areas—ruins, tourist facilities, and attendance. A typical ranger-led party is shown above.

David Mathias

November 17, 1963 ● EMPIRE MAGAZINE

12

MESA VERDE NATIONAL PARK

Map shows roughly the old and new Indian ruins areas, and roads planned to bring them all in easy reach of Mesa Verde visitors.

George Cattanach, archeologist in new Wetherill Mesa area, has a historical jig-saw puzzle of broken pottery to fit together.

The Denver Post ● November 17, 1963

BIG changes are in the making for Mesa Verde National Park. All over the country there is new interest in the American Indian. Tie this to an explosive population increase, the growing affluence of the American people, and widespread interest in the new Four Corners Highway—the Navajo Trail—and you set the stage for a much expanded interest in Mesa Verde National Park, which lies alongside the new transcontinental route.

Mesa Verde—Spanish for "green table"—is a large plateau rising 1,500 to 2,000 feet above surrounding valleys. It was the home of Pueblo Indians for more than 12 centuries and is famous for its well-preserved cliff dwellings set into shallow caves in the canyon walls. It is now a national park entirely within the Colorado borders. The park entrance lies 10 miles east of Cortez and 38 miles west of Durango on U. S. Highway 160. From the park entrance it is 21 miles south to the present Park Headquarters.

The casual visitor can view the cliff dwellings from overlooks. The more curious and hardy can take, in good weather, ranger-guided tours along narrow trails and up and down steep ladders right into the dwellings themselves. A museum offers tremendous interest to the curious.

Signs of change at Mesa Verde were not readily apparent this past summer, but change is on the way. Spruce Tree Lodge, the informal hotel located in the heart of the park, overflowed daily during the regular season. Daytime visitors may not have felt crowded, but those who stayed overnight were likely to.

The "all campsites occupied" sign went up at the park entrance nearly every evening. An estimated 200 to 300 cars were turned away almost nightly. The on-site tents and cabins of Spruce Tree Lodge were filled, and in the four camping areas of Mesa Verde vacationers were stacked as tightly as clothespins in a row. At meals lunch counters and diningrooms were filled and lines of hungry people waited their turns to sit down.

PUBLIC INTEREST ROCKETS

Chester A. Thomas, superintendent of Mesa Verde National Park, gives figures to show how interest has boomed.

Attendance this year at the park, from Jan. 1 through Oct. 17, was 311,392. Last year for the same period it was 251,841—and 1962 was a record year. The increase was 59,551, or 23.6 per cent.

Growth of business in the overnight campgrounds is also impressive. In the Jan. 1-Oct. 17 period this year 97,667 stayed overnight, compared with 81,331 in the same period last year.

Mesa Verde is open the year [...] with the facilities available [...] on the weather.

"As long as the weather is good and we have weeks of real mild weather we continue to offer the ranger tours, using Spruce Tree [...] says Thomas, "And our visitors [...] freely visit the museum."

This museum is at park headquarters and its exhibits tell the story of the Mesa Verde people. It [...] crafts and industries. It's free [...] open from 8 a. m. to 5 p. m. during the "off" season.

Spruce Tree ruin is in the canyon behind the museum. It is the best preserved in Mesa Verde and contains 114 living rooms and eight ceremonial rooms, called kivas.

"When the bad weather comes," Thomas says, "we have to discontinue the ranger tours. But when it clears and the snow and mud go away, we start them again as long as there are enough visitors to warrant them."

TRIPS FOR BAD WEATHER

In any event the road into headquarters from U. S. Highway 160 is open eight hours a day. And the [...] mile loop trip—called the Mesa Verde Loop—offers many good views of the dwellings, even if the guided tours are temporarily halted.

Crowded conditions of [...] ing will be ended one of these [...] Thomas promises, by Mesa Verde [...] participation in a general National Parks improvement program known as Mission 66.

The "66" is derived from the original plan to complete the improvements in 1966. However the target date for Mesa Verde is now [...]

Thomas says.

Mesa Verde's part in the plan includes a virtual doubling of the facilities at the park, rebuilding of the lodge and headquarters on new sites, and the opening of an entirely new section of Indian ruins and dwellings on the Wetherill Mesa near the present well-known dwellings in the Chapin Mesa area.

The ruins and dwellings to be available on Wetherill Mesa will not differ in great manner or degree from the ones on view in the present Chapin Mesa area.

This is not to imply that the houses, Pueblo ruins and cliff dwellings at Wetherill will not be just as interesting as those now on view, or that they will not be different to the viewer. It is planned, however, that the visitor who sees one complex of ruins will see a satisfying and complete sample of the intensely interesting homes of the vanished Indian people who once inhabited Mesa Verde.

This autumn, three major cliff dwellings on Wetherill Mesa—Long House, Mug House, and Step House—have been fully excavated and stabilized. In addition five pueblos on top of the mesa have been completed. The Wetherill Mesa project will include a museum, trails, interpretative [...]

62

National Park Service was heralded as a "renaissance" for the service, which needed to play catch-up from the wartime cutbacks and the clamor of the automobile-visiting public. Mission 66 was in full swing in Mesa Verde by 1960 and eventually resulted in construction of the Far View Visitor Center, Far View Lodge, Morefield Campground, and the opening of Wetherill Mesa to visitation. These developments were aimed at providing park visitors with an alternative to the congested Spruce Tree Point and other increasingly battered sites on Chapin Mesa, notably Cliff Palace, Spruce Tree House, and Balcony House.

Meanwhile, in 1957 a major transportation milestone was marked with the closure of the Knife Edge Road and the opening of a shorter, safer route to Chapin Mesa. The newer, twenty-mile road, which visitors travel today to enter the park, included a tunnel that at the time was the longest highway tunnel in Colorado.

Into the 1960s, visitation continued to set records. In 1963, 320,000 visitors came—an annual record for the park—and in November of that year reporter Edwin P.

Hoyt wrote an overly optimistic feature for the *Denver Post*'s *Empire Magazine* about changes gleaming on Mesa Verde's horizon due to Mission 66:

> Signs of change at Mesa Verde were not readily apparent this past summer, but change is on the way. Spruce Tree Lodge, the informal hotel located in the heart of the park, overflowed daily during the regular season. Daytime visitors may not have felt crowded, but those who stayed overnight were likely to.
>
> The "all campsites occupied" sign went up at the park entrance nearly every evening. An estimated 200 to 300 cars were turned away almost nightly. The on-site tents and cabins of Spruce Tree Lodge were filled, and in the four camping areas of Mesa Verde vacationers were stacked as tightly as clothespins in a row. At meals, lunch counters and dining rooms were filled and lines of hungry people waited their turns to sit down. …
>
> Crowded conditions of summer visiting will be ended one of these days, [Superintendent Chester] Thomas promises, by Mesa Verde's participation in a general National Parks improvement program known as Mission 66.
>
> The "66" is derived from the original plan to complete the improvements in 1966. However, the target date for Mesa Verde is now 1967, Thomas says.
>
> Mesa Verde's part in the plan includes a virtual doubling of all the facilities at the park, rebuilding of the lodge and headquarters at new sites, and the opening of an entirely new section of Indian ruins and dwellings on the Wetherill Mesa. …
>
> This autumn, three major cliff dwellings on Wetherill Mesa—Long House, Mug House, and Step House—have been fully excavated and stabilized. In addition five pueblos on top of the mesa have been completed.

A tunnel permitting safer travel along the park entrance road was completed in 1957.

CHAPTER 5

TOURISM AND WORLDWIDE RECOGNITION

It did not take long for the wonders of Mesa Verde to become one of the wonders of the world. From its earliest days, Mesa Verde has beckoned foreign travelers as well as stateside tourists. Starting most notably with Gustaf Nordenskiöld, visitors have come, toured, and often written accounts of what they saw and felt.

With the park's popularity came economic windfall to every community and county surrounding Mesa Verde. Some towns, indeed, have come to depend on park visitors for their very lifeblood. From the beginning there has been competition among Cortez, Mancos, and Durango to dominate the trade, and even Santa Fe, Denver, Flagstaff, and Gallup have joined the rivalry.

Mesa Verde draws people from around the globe for its cultural and natural treasures. As a tribute to its unique qualities, the park was declared a World Cultural Heritage Site in 1978. But Mesa Verde's popularity comes with a price: it is possible to love the park to death. The park's budget could barely keep pace, and the challenge of preserving this irreplaceable heritage grows larger with every year.

LOVING THE PARK TO DEATH

At the end of World War II, Americans reveled in a postwar boom. Mesa Verde's visitation reflected that release of pent-up energy, money, and leisure time. In 1952, 100,000 visitors came to the park; eight years later that number had doubled.

By July 1965, Mesa Verde posted another milestone—a dubious one to be sure. Some 100,000 people visited the park in a single month. Superintendent Chester Thomas declared that Balcony House had reached the "breaking point," and it would be mandatory to limit trips into the site the following summer. Because Americans were in such a rush to get on to their next destination, Thomas felt this would be a self-limiting act, for people would not wish to wait and take their "turn" to go in. Cliff Palace had become a "solid mass of milling humanity," and Thomas's 1965 annual report painted a picture of "bedlam" there:

> With hundreds of people per hour and rangers being forced to yell above the racket, interpretation at this site is rapidly becoming a farce. The cave acts as a sounding board

OPPOSITE: Spruce Tree House has always been one of the most popular cliff dwellings in Mesa Verde.

Visitors to Long House climb ladders much as the ancestral residents did. Park managers struggle to provide an authentic experience while protecting the integrity of the fragile archaeological sites.

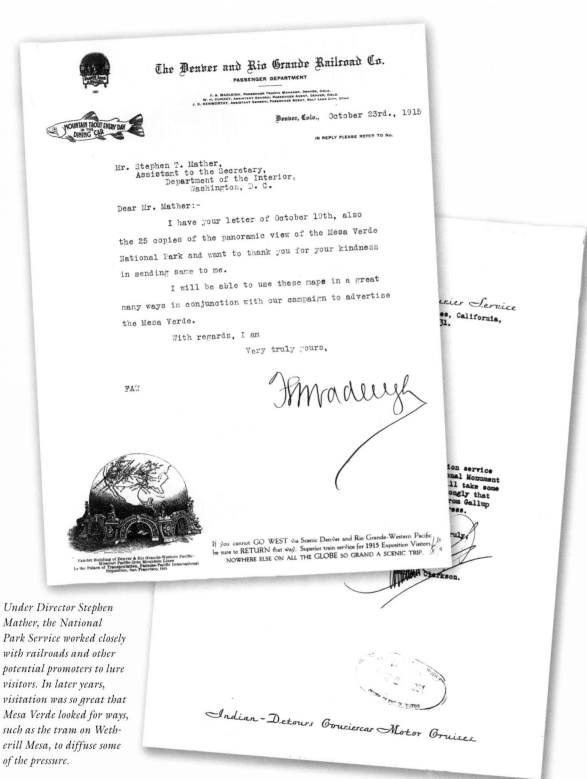

for scuffling feet, wails of crying kids, the rangers' voices; bedlam is the rule of the day all summer long. We may be forced to limit interpretation to what can be accomplished at the "viewpoint," station men at intervals across the front of the ruin, and allow people to visit the site without having to wait for guided trips. We have learned from Spruce Tree House that few people will pay any attention to the numbered "stations" in the site or refer to their guidebooks, so making Cliff Palace self-guiding is out. Self-guiding is not a device for use in ruins unless forced into it as we were at Spruce Tree House to try and give the short-term visitor something. …

The problem of "milling humanity" described by Thomas did not improve as the park entered the 1970s. Mesa Verde was being "loved to death." A ticket system was instituted for Cliff Palace and Balcony House to try to regulate visitation at those popular sites, and in 1973 Wetherill Mesa finally opened to visitors. The Mesa Verde Company ran a tram out from Far View to the newly developed Wetherill Mesa sites. The idea was to relieve pressure on the increasingly overrun sites

Under Director Stephen Mather, the National Park Service worked closely with railroads and other potential promoters to lure visitors. In later years, visitation was so great that Mesa Verde looked for ways, such as the tram on Wetherill Mesa, to diffuse some of the pressure.

72

Sept 15-20.

of Florence to build a fire with
the use of matches + gasoline?
Answer:
One hour + 35 minutes by the
watch, + it happened on Monarch Pass

Ralph J. Wann
Canon City Colo.

We don't know whether it was tea
or not — perhaps the altitude —
but our friend Ralph Wann of
Canon City grew much younger —
at least he gained young
ideas after two hours at Spruce
Tree Camp

Sept 16 1921

"Silently one by one"
hewn and cut and carried
Ex amples of Faith + Patience
Their Building blocks string square
Structures of finest masonry
Let us look well at them
That we learn the Success True
Building up right and square.

Robert C. Burt
Sept 17/1921

"Worth While"

73

Mesa Verde
Oct 1921
Three miles and rain
we've climbed the trail
O'er mountains, valleys
hill and dale —
A whole days ride —
A trip worth while
When we made
The engine "bite."

Bernice Jay Clovis N. Mex
Marian H. Ream Durango Colo
Ethel Davis Cruddeman Durango.
Edwin P Wilson,
Vereene L. Garrett Brookfield Mo.

Oct. 8, 1921.

Back To Mesa Verde for the second time —
will there be a third? Evelyn and I are beginning
to realize that perhaps it is best we didn't come as
"Paint" and "Patsy" Could we have made it?
Sure! When you want a thing bad enough, you can
always get it — or doit—
Evelyn & Dorothy,
Tazwell Co.
Washington, Ill.

Over the past century, visitors have seen Mesa Verde in various ways. There have been many famous visitors to the park, including the Crown Prince and Princess of Sweden in 1924 (bottom row, center). Today, proper etiquette in sites would not include sitting on the rock walls.

From 1969 until 1983, luminarias were lit inside the rooms of Spruce Tree House on winter nights. Though it was a highly popular tradition among visitors, the practice is now limited to once a year during the holidays to minimize impact on the fragile cliff dwellings.

on Chapin Mesa. Still, people kept coming. In 1976, the nation's bicentennial year, park visitation hit an all-time high of 676,935. Park administrators were even considering putting a quota on the number of visitors allowed to enter a site each hour, but abandoned the idea.

Some changes in the mid-1980s might have been subtle to visitors but were important from an administrative standpoint. In 1989, following an environmental assessment and a two-year trial run, the park announced the end of the concessionaire-operated tram service to Wetherill Mesa and instead opened the road to private vehicles.

Once at Wetherill Mesa, visitors then boarded a mini-tram for the four-mile tour of sites that included Long House, the second largest cliff dwelling in Mesa Verde. This change was all part of an ongoing effort to try to redistribute some of the crowds from Chapin to Wetherill Mesa. And while Wetherill is an incredible place to visit, and the latest arrangement presented a reasonable way to do so, for some reason this part of the park still does not lure as many visitors as planners had hoped.

Through the years, an array of books and pamphlets has been published and distributed to Mesa Verde visitors. They show a fascinating evolution in design styles and changes in appeals to the public's attention.

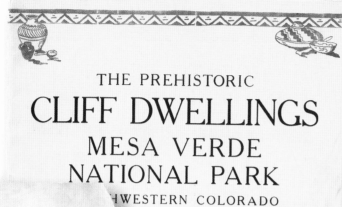

THE PREHISTORIC
CLIFF DWELLINGS
MESA VERDE
NATIONAL PARK
HWESTERN COLORADO

Charles B. Kelly
MANCOS, COLORADO

Spruce Tree House, Mesa Verde National Park

Outfitter and Guide to the Famous
Cliff Dweller Ruins
Of the Mesa Verde National Park

Ancient Ruins
of the
Southwest

2761

REMARKA
CIENT HA
E UNITE

MESA
VERDE
NATIONAL
PARK
COLORADO

D&RGWRR
ROYAL
GORGE
ROUTE
SCENIC LINE

© Colorado Historical Society

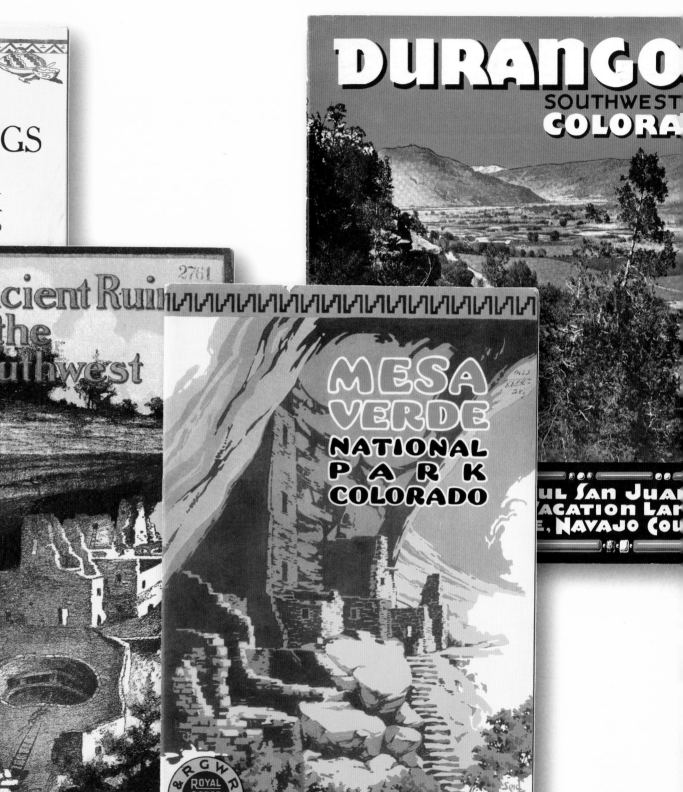

DURANGO
SOUTHWEST
COLORA

ul San Juan
ACATION Lan
E, NAVAJO Cou

70

DEAR ANCESTORS ...

Besides the normal wear and tear of time, Mesa Verde's archaeological sites also suffer from vandalism and illegal removal of objects by visitors. In order for archaeologists to most effectively study past cultures, they must view artifacts within the context of their original location, a situation some visitors don't understand or choose to disregard. Many people, feeling remorse, return the pilfered items to the park, along with a brief, often handwritten note or letter. The park keeps these letters and the potsherds, corncobs, or other artifacts that were taken. Here are a few of the letters, complete with creative spellings, indicating the strong motivator of guilt that led to the return of the objects.

To Mesa Verde Park Service

Twenty years ago I had the opportunity to visit your park. In a sense of adventure I climbed down to one of the cliff ledges. I removed a piece of corn & some mud with corn husks that were laying around some boulders. In a sense of contrition I am now returning these items with my apology. I just was not thinking at the time that if everyone took a piece of the Anasazi history there would be none left.

Dear Sir:

Recently I visited your park and became so intrigued with the Anasazi mystique that I purchased these pottery fragments from a store in your area. While I believe the store owners are within the law, (I assumed these fragments were obtained legally—the store is near the park) I am no longer comfortable owning them. I understand a number of groups are trying to prevent scavenging for historical and religious purposes.

I know now, that I do not have to own pieces of this mystery, to call it my own.

To Whom It May Concern:

I thought I was creating a memory—A piece of history—something to write home about—I was wrong to deface my ancesters' heritage—Luck—I've had better—Please accept this with my apologies.

Take these rocks back the spirits can have them I've had enough bad luck and bad things happen to my family its time for a change

dear ancestors

i felt the obligation to return these pot-chards to their place of origin my apologies for taking something that was not mine to take.

Recently I was reading the *National Geographic* Magazine and ran across an article that explained how tons of petrified wood taken from the Petrified Forest in Arizona were being returned by people who realized the importance of preserving our parks for future generations. I realized then that I was one of those people who had disregarded efforts to preserve our parks. ... I am returning the enclosed artifacts that I took during a visit to Mesa Verde several years ago. Please accept my apology and the enclosed artifacts as an indication of an effort to restore my respect for our parks and natural resources.

THE NATION'S FIRST WORLD CULTURAL HERITAGE SITE

On September 8, 1978, Mesa Verde National Park received a high honor. It was declared the nation's first World Cultural Heritage Site by the United Nations Educational, Scientific and Cultural Organization (UNESCO). It was among twelve sites in seven countries throughout the world that received the special international recognition. UNESCO's World Heritage Committee selects "cultural heritage properties" that may be

> either monuments, groups of buildings, or sites which are of outstanding universal value from the historical, ethnological, anthropological, or purely aesthetic point of view, or a combination of these. Mesa Verde National Park is unique in the world in that it possesses all of these values at one site. Thus it is eminently qualified to be designated as a World Heritage Site. ...

Three years later, on June 29, 1981, Mesa Verde marked its seventy-fifth anniversary as a national park and simultaneously was officially dedicated as a World Cultural Heritage Site. The ceremony began at 10:30 A.M. with the national anthem, an invocation, introductions and remarks, traditional Navajo social dance songs, a keynote speech by National Park Service Director Russell Dickenson, and a reception in the museum.

The program prepared for the event stated:

> Mesa Verde National Park, through the perseverance of the Colorado Cliff Dwellers [sic] Association, was established by Congress on June 29, 1906, " ... for the preservation from injury or spoilation of the ruins and other works and relics of prehistoric or primitive man within said park ... with a view to increasing the knowledge of such objects and aiding the general advancement of archaeological science."

The most significant archaeological reserve in the United

THROUGH THE COLLECTIVE RECOGNITION OF THE COMMUNITY OF NATIONS
EXPRESSED WITHIN THE PRINCIPLES OF THE
CONVENTION CONCERNING PROTECTION OF THE WORLD
CULTURAL AND NATURAL HERITAGE

MESA VERDE NATIONAL PARK

HAS BEEN DESIGNATED A

WORLD HERITAGE SITE

AND JOINS A SELECT LIST OF PROTECTED AREAS
AROUND THE WORLD WHOSE OUTSTANDING NATURAL AND CULTURAL RESOURCES
FORM THE COMMON INHERITANCE OF ALL MANKIND

SEPTEMBER 8, 1978

A plaque observes Mesa Verde's designation as a World Heritage Site; in 1981 Mesa Verde celebrated that honor along with its seventy-fifth anniversary. Rangers hosted an international audience, including a delegation from China.

States, Mesa Verde is unique in both national and international scope. It is the first and only National Park in the system dedicated to the works of prehistoric man.

As leaders in the conservation and historic preservation movement, it is the mission of the National Park Service to preserve and protect for the nation not only the natural environment but our cultural heritage as well.

Mesa Verde National Park was designated a World Heritage Cultural Site by the United Nations Educational, Scientific and Cultural Organization (UNESCO) on September 8, 1978. As Mesa Verde celebrates the 75th anniversary of its inclusion in the National Park System, it is quite appropriate that we gather together here to dedicate the park as a World Heritage Site.

THE FIRST WORLD CONFERENCE ON CULTURAL PARKS

Mesa Verde's importance as a cultural treasure was further recognized six years later when it was chosen to host the First World Conference on Cultural Parks. Nearly 200 professionals from some forty countries attended— among them archaeologists, historians, lawyers, planners, and native people—and engaged in discussions of the philosophical and ethical questions related to preservation. The conference was dedicated to Gustaf Nordenskiöld for the "first conscious attempt to systematically excavate and record the archeology of the Mesa Verde plateau." In the keynote address, then-director of the National Park Service Russell Dickenson declared that, "Surely Mesa Verde National Park is a most appropriate place, at least in the United States, for us to meet and share experiences and concerns for the management, conservation, and public use of cultural resources." We have a "moral imperative," he went on, to identify, protect, and perpetuate "these special places."

Mark Michel, president of the nonprofit Archaeological Conservancy based in Santa Fe, New Mexico, spoke of a concept of managing cultural resources in national parks in the United States set forth in a 1980 federal law that applied to Chaco Canyon south of Mesa Verde. In Michel's view, the legislation was significant because it recognized for the first time that culture was the crucial element, not just impressive structures. In his opinion, Mesa Verde was one of the first places where this "vastly improved policy" should be implemented, to tell the broader story beyond the confines of the national park itself:

Visitors from all over the world come to see the spectacular ruins around us, but recent and not-so-recent information suggests that the ruins in this park are only a fraction of the extent of the Mesa Verde culture. In fact, archeologists now believe that ten times as many people (4,000 on the mesa and 40,000 in the valley) were living in the Montezuma Valley near Cortez at the base of Mesa Verde as were living in the park at the peak of the culture around A.D. 1250.

A number of these people were apparently living in great Mesa Verde towns in the valley, many of which appear to have more ruins and more kivas than all of the ruins in the park combined. But they were not included in the park because many of the most spectacular of these ruins are located on private lands and because the valley ruins lack the spectacular setting of the great cliff dwellings. (By chance, two of the valley ruins were preserved by the National Park Service as other units and several more have legal protection because they are on federal land.)

No significant research has yet taken place on the great Mesa Verde towns of the valley, and many have been severely damaged by looters and development. But it is impossible to understand what is going on here in the park without an understanding of the great Mesa Verde towns of the valley. Furthermore, there is clear evidence in some of the valley towns of a Chacoan presence 150 years before the height of the Mesa Verde culture. The relationship between these two great cultures is a subject that is little understood today, largely because the sites where the two cultures overlap the most are not a part of either park.

Clearly our understanding of the ruins in the park is

severely limited by the lack of knowledge of the ruins in the valley. The visitor is being short-changed because he or she is seeing only a very small part of a much bigger, more complex picture. A true "Mesa Verde National Park" would encompass the ruins in the valley as well as the spectacular cliff dwellings. This has many practical advantages as well. Research sites are virtually nonexistent on the mesa since most were fully excavated years ago. A new interpretive site would tend to alleviate overcrowding in the park and extend the length of the visitor season. …

If the concept of culture-wide parks is widely adopted, there will be ample resources for new research for centuries to come. And this continuing research is crucial to enlightened interpretation.

THE CHALLENGES OF PRESERVATION

In June 1998 the National Trust for Historic Preservation listed Mesa Verde among America's eleven most endangered historic places. Fire, erosion, and the park service's scant budget allocations for preservation were cited as reasons for this ignominious recognition. In its June 21 Sunday edition, the *Denver Post* sounded the alarm in a strongly worded editorial decrying the park's plight as a "disaster in the making." Though the editorial writers for the state's largest newspaper may have been guilty of slight hyperbole, the fact is that archaeological sites all over Mesa Verde are deteriorating, and the park service backlog remains an urgent matter.

Coloradans should feel alarmed by threats facing the irreplaceable, world-renowned historic resource that's virtually outside their back porch. Twice now, the magnificent and haunting Mesa Verde National Park … has been labeled as endangered . …

In 1978 Mesa Verde became the first U.S. location designated by the United Nations as a World Heritage Cultural Site. "From the U.N.'s global perspective, it may be the most important historic site in this country," historian Tom Noel wrote.

So while Colorado doesn't have the Egyptian Pyramids or the Great Wall of China, it does have Mesa Verde—with its 4,500 archaeological sites and 2 million artifacts.

But many of the park's treasures are at risk of being lost forever.

Last week, the National Trust for Historic Preservation included Mesa Verde on its list of Most Endangered Places. Last year, the World Monuments Fund also called Mesa Verde one of the 100 most endangered historic sites in the United States.

While the park service safely maintains Mesa Verde's major tourist attractions, it hasn't even looked at hundreds of other archaeological sites in 50 years—if just to make sure the places haven't fallen down or been washed away. Ancient plaster in the well-known cliff dwellings has been deteriorating. A fire two years ago burned 5,000 acres in the park, searing ancient petroglyphs.

The potential loss is a disaster in the making.

By the late 1990s, threats facing the park were drawing the attention of editorial writers.

Park service employees have undertaken near-heroic efforts to preserve Mesa Verde's resources.

But there's not enough money to do the whole job properly—not enough staff, equipment, or scientific research. While the National Park Service gave Mesa Verde a modest budget increase and let it keep 80 percent of the money raised from last year's entrance fee hike, the increases haven't adequately addressed the problem.

Simply put, Mesa Verde could serve as a poster child for why Congress absolutely must correct the $5 billion maintenance backlog throughout America's national park system. And its plight underscores the pressing need for more private and foundation aid for the national parks.

If America lets Mesa Verde's pre-Columbian wonders crumble, it will have betrayed history and sinned against future generations.

A WORLD WONDER

In October 1999, *National Geographic Traveler* magazine published a "Special Collector's Issue," in which it listed fifty wonders of the world that have "managed to stand the test of time," places that share traits of "universal cultural relevance … soaring artistry … inventiveness … sheer physical magnitude." Mesa Verde was among the fifty, which also included the Taj Mahal, Vatican City, Acropolis, Petra, Machu Picchu, the Great Wall, Angkor, the Pyramids, and even cyberspace. Poet, novelist, and nonfiction author Evan S. Connell penned this tribute to Mesa Verde in the magazine:

The long green table, Mesa Verde, stands a thousand feet above the Montezuma Valley in southwestern Colorado. Its colors, in fact, are not merely juniper green but olive, sage, burnt umber, sienna, russet, and similar high desert modulations—if one ignores bright little explosions of flowers. Overhead, suffusing everything, an immense Western sky. Except for ancient stone-and-mortar cliff houses stuck to precipitous canyon walls there is scarcely a building in sight. What prevails throughout the national park is a feeling that one must be near the rim of the world.

In 1888 a rancher looking for stray cattle noticed an apartment house clinging to a canyon wall. He and his brother-in-law found a way up and explored the rooms, leaving fresh boot tracks in centuries of dust. Here and there lay sandals, arrows, baskets, stone axes, painted clay mugs, seed jars, ladles, bowls, metates, and other household goods—as if the people had only stepped out and might return at any moment.

During the next several decades almost 600 cliff dwellings were discovered. The tallest building stood 86 feet high and had 80 rooms. Cliff Palace, the largest, held 151 rooms and 23 circular kivas—these being subsurface chambers used for religious discussion and sometimes by men who perhaps just wanted to get away from the wife.

Not long ago an East Coast friend of mine decided to visit Santa Fe. The provincial Southwest rather bored him; nonetheless, I proposed a tour of Mesa Verde. As we drove up the narrow curling road through evergreens, past variegated bluffs, he did not say much. We drove to the highest point and looked around. There was a hawk sailing the current, mesas, canyons, purple shadows, nothing else for about a thousand miles. Near the park's museum we sat on a bench and looked down at a creamy ruin called Spruce Tree House. There were slowly moving shadows, sunlight on disintegrating walls, and the mysterious aura of people seven centuries gone. My eastern friend did not move or speak for half an hour. Now he wants to come back.

In 1999, First Lady Hillary Clinton visited the park to launch the Save America's Treasures program. Native Americans welcomed her, and she received an award from National Park Service Director Robert Stanton.

SAVE AMERICA'S TREASURES

Pleas for funding apparently did not fall on deaf ears. In 1999, the federal government came through with substantial assistance for Mesa Verde. In May, then–first lady Hillary Rodham Clinton visited the park to present a sizable grant as part of the Save America's Treasures project, a public-private effort between the White House Millennium Council and the National Trust for Historic Preservation. Mrs. Clinton announced a $1.5 million grant to the park, matched by an equal sum in private funds, in what was eventually to grow into a $10 million site conservation program in the park over six years. Nearly 600 sites, including the park's "crown jewel" cliff dwellings, were to be inventoried, their conditions assessed, and if necessary work done to prevent further damage. The park service's Julie Bell was in charge of the conditions assessment portion, while park archaeologist Joel Brisbin oversaw new work in Spruce Tree House, which followed the same techniques as Larry Nordby's work in Cliff Palace.

77

CHAPTER 6

NATURAL HISTORY: MESA VERDE'S WILD SIDE

By the 1930s, America's national parks already had a good record for interpreting natural history to the visiting public. Mesa Verde, with its obvious archaeological emphasis, was sometimes overlooked as a "natural history" park. Yet there is a wealth of flora and fauna on the mesa, from bighorn sheep, mule deer, and elk to dense piñon-juniper forests, rare marine fossils, and unusual endemic insects. These many valuable resources require thoughtful management, and since the park's earliest days, scientists, interpreters, and administrators have worked to preserve and protect Mesa Verde's many natural wonders.

THE FIRST NATURALISTS

As Mesa Verde gained popularity, visitors used to the rich natural history of national parks such as Yellowstone and Yosemite began to want more from the park than its archaeological story. In addition to Mesa Verde's unique cultural history, there was also a 90 million-year natural history story to tell. Thus in 1930, Paul Franke became Mesa Verde's first ranger-naturalist. It was his job to interpret the park's natural and cultural resources to visitors, and he also established the Mesa Verde Library Association, now the Mesa Verde Museum Association, to help support park interpretation. In the charmingly homespun *Mesa Verde Notes*, Franke and others shared observations as they traveled through the park. A fascinating entry titled "Mountain Lion Action," written by Chief Ranger Carlisle Crouch, appeared in the December 1934 issue of the *Notes*. Crouch's spelling has been maintained here.

> Mountain lions … have been observed at infrequent intervals in the Mesa Verde, but in most instances it was just a fleeting glimpse when one would cross the highway in front of an automobile's lights. So it was with unusual interest I witnessed one of the big cats in action in the day light. The activity observed seemed as extrordinary to me as the opportunity to observe it. It appeared inconsistent for this large animal to engage in stalking prairie dogs … in this region where mule deer … are comparatively abundant, and to carry on this activity in a relatively open canyon in the day time.
>
> The hour of the day was early 8:30 in the morning, and the sun was out bright and warm on this fourth of November when I began a hike down Prater Canyon. … The canyon at this point is open and flat, and innumerable prairie dogs have taken up homesteads in it. The trail follows the west wall, and low ridges at several points conceal it from the open canyon floor. From one of these ridges, I saw the lion out in the canyon in the midst of his maneuvers, so seeing a concealed vantage point I watched the activity.
>
> The lion's massive body was crouching just back of the dirt mound pulled up, by the prairie dog in digging its subterranean den, much in the same manner as a house cat just before it springs on its prey. Endless patience must have

OPPOSITE: Artist Larry Eifert's interpretation of Mesa Verde's flora and fauna. This painting may be seen in the Chapin Mesa Archeological Museum.

Mesa Verde Notes *contained nuggets of cultural and natural information about the park.*

been required for this position, for the dogs are very sensitive to the presence of any "foreingner" in their colony. One dog was an unsuspecting little creature on this occasion, however, for I saw it slowly and cautiously emerge from his den only to be snatched by the right paw of his much superior contemporary.

At this point I made some noise, in my eagerness to approach closer, and the King of the Mesa Verde canyons trotted away to his rocky cliffs.

In the first half of the twentieth century, a number of Mesa Verde's rangers performed natural history work, contributing a great deal to the park's knowledge base and specimen collections. The first botanists in the park were Dean Bader and Hazel Schmoll. Some of their collections from the 1920s are still found in the park herbarium. Working for the park's chief naturalist in 1935, wildlife technician Chas Quaintance conducted extensive field surveys of wildlife and other natural features in the park that year with contributions from Harold Pratt. During the 1940s, some of the earliest bird surveys and the mounting of bird specimens were carried out by ranger-naturalists Jean Pinkley and Don Watson. From the mid-1940s through much of the 1950s, Donald Spencer from the U.S. Fish and Wildlife Service was assigned to work at Mesa Verde to study the overpopulation of porcupine. These surveys, studies, and collection activities helped lay the foundation for understanding Mesa Verde's rich natural history.

Marilyn Colyer, Mesa Verde's first biological science technician, pioneered the study of the park's natural history. For more than forty years, she has worked in the park, providing the basis of much of what we know today about plants and animals. She began working in the park in 1963 on the Wetherill project, then became a full-time naturalist in the early 1970s. Her field research includes studying the habits and habitats of the park's wildlife, monitoring their activities, and conducting surveys to better understand their populations. She has bolstered her field research with oral histories conducted with many local residents, capturing valuable knowledge about past environmental conditions in and around the park. Colyer is not the first natural historian to study the park's resources, but she has made great contributions through her comprehensive investigations. She also enlists helpers, from volunteers to research scientists. Marilyn's research will give future park managers a firm foundation for conserving Mesa Verde's natural treasures.

ANIMALS INSIDE AND OUT

Of concern during the first half of the twentieth century at parks throughout the West, including Mesa Verde, was heavy, unregulated grazing by cattle and sheep, which was allowed on public lands, national park or otherwise. In addition to open-range grazing, in its early years the park also had several private holdings within its boundaries, including Prater, Morefield, Whites, and Mancos Canyons. Early superintendents made buying out these grazing operations a high priority. Once inholdings were purchased and open-range grazing in the park ended, dozens of miles of livestock fencing were built, forming a boundary to keep cattle, sheep, and feral horses out.

Later in the century, concern turned from domesticated animals to endemic populations. In 1966 the high density of mule deer outstripping the capacity of the range prompted park managers to propose a 25 percent reduction of the herd. A controversy arose over who should do the killing—park rangers only or sport hunters—and that led to a study of Mesa Verde's mule deer. In 1967, research teams from Colorado State University began looking at deer numbers, movements, and overall health both of the animals and their range. (Mule deer migrate in and out of the park each year, arriving in March and April and going down to lower elevations in winter when snow is deep.)

In the study's first year, more than a hundred deer were tagged with collars and colored ribbons on their ears. When the study began, there were an estimated 4,500 to 5,200 deer in summer and fall; by 1976, only about one-fourth of that number remained. The researchers concluded that this drastic population decline was underway even as they began the project, and that heavy browsing of the range was the likely cause for the initial drop. But as the habitat improved, the deer herd continued to decline.

A high death rate among fawns was the immediate reason, which the researchers speculated was due to predators, primarily coyotes, bobcats, and the occasional mountain lion. This was not normal, and in their final report the researchers noted that "special circumstances" occurred at Mesa Verde that let predators temporarily, but significantly, influence the population of their prey. They wrote:

We postulate that as the size of the deer population slowly increased to unprecedented levels so did the size of their predator population (predator control has never been practiced at Mesa Verde National Park). Predators did not exert an appreciable impact on the deer herd until, relatively suddenly, the deer population began to decline as a result of range overutilization. At least several years are required before a predator population can fully adjust to such a change and reestablish its former balance with its prey population. During this period, often referred to as the "predator lag period," the predator population exists in a state of relative overabundance and can further depress the already declining prey population by taking a greater than usual proportion of the fawn crop. We believe that our research was conducted during this period when "predator lag" was exerting a strong secondary effect in accentuating and prolonging the population decline.

If this hypothesis is correct, the outlook for the mule deer

Mule deer in Mesa Verde were the topic of intensive studies in past years.

of Mesa Verde National Park is very optimistic. ... The deer are now in good physical condition and their range is well along the way toward recovery from previous damage. A population decline was needed and appears to have served its purpose.

As with most other national parks during this era, "varmints," such as prairie dogs and even tent caterpillars, were regularly targeted for control or elimination. As one example, Mesa Verde undertook a campaign against tree-chewing porcupines. In his 1932 report on the porcupine problem, ranger C. R. Markley wrote:

Since I can mention nothing in favor of the porcupine, this report deals entirely with his evils. I have tried to present the evidence with which I accuse the rodent and which I hope will convict him, so that his numbers can be materially reduced ... Mesa Verde has long been famous for its beautiful stand of evergreen trees, its very name is Spanish for green tableland—this all important forest must be protected against all enemies.

There was a sometimes-confusing dichotomy between species that were perceived as good or bad. So even in this "cultural park," managing nature turned out to be a full-time job for a great many people.

WILDERNESS

By the second half of the twentieth century, Mesa Verde's natural resources were achieving a higher profile, often driven by national programs. In the 1960s, Park Mesa was declared a national "Research Natural Area," and was slated for scientific study and left unaltered by humans. In the 1970s, 42,900 acres of the park were surveyed as "roadless." In compliance with the Wilderness Act, Mesa

Verde was required to evaluate its roadless areas for wilderness designation. Yet park administrators opposed any wilderness in the park, fearing it could interfere with future development plans or archaeological excavations. In 1976, a compromise was reached with wilderness advocates in which 8,500 acres of the park's steep northern and eastern escarpments would be given wilderness status.

WILDFIRE

In the wooded West, the threat of wildfire is always a serious matter. Fortunately, during the park's first fifty-three years, long before modern fire suppression technology was available, Mesa Verde experienced only one severe fire season: 1934. During the week of July 10 of that year, two wildfires started burning on Wild Horse Mesa and in Wickiup Canyon. The Civilian Conservation Corps (CCC), whose duty it was to suppress all fires in the park, got a quick immersion into the real world of firefighting that summer, working to safeguard the mesa's dense piñon-juniper forest and protect archaeological sites and modern buildings from fire. In a report filed in October 1934, the fire control efforts were relayed in dramatic, moment-by-moment description:

When [firefighters] arrived at the major fire at 3:15 PM, after a six mile hike over rough canyons and brushy ridges, it was seen to be on Wickiup Mesa between West Wickiup Canyon and Long Canyon, covering an area of about 600 acres. Immediately a fire break was started around the north and west sides to check any further advance in that direction, the wind being from the southeast.

Shortly after work was begun the wind switched to the northwest and started the flames to burning back on themselves, which aided materially in their control. ...

[Additional crews arrived, an emergency supply camp was set up, and trucks managed to get in. Exhausted after two nonstop days, the crews received relief on July 13, and the fire was thought to be sufficiently under control. Meanwhile, the fire on Wild Horse Mesa had broken out again and was spreading rapidly.]

... by 10:00 AM Saturday, July 14, it was evident that something was wrong, for a high wind had come up from the southwest and the fire seemed to be spreading north and east. All available men at the ECW camp and Park Headquarters were called out and rushed to the scene. By 1:00 PM the fire was a raging furnace nearly five miles in length and advancing east toward Park Headquarters at race horse speed. The fire at that time had covered the north part of Wetherill Mesa and was advancing down into Long Canyon.

The only recourse then to assure protection for the Park Headquarters area was to build a wide fire trail down Wickiup Mesa from the North Rim, and join it into the north end of the Wickiup Mesa burned area of the fire of July 11, this trail being about one and one-half miles in length. This was quite an undertaking with a tired crew. ...

Saturday morning, July 14, when the fire was seen to be out of control additional help was asked from the outside, and at 7:30 PM Saturday night the first crew of eighty-four Navajos arrived from Shiprock, New Mexico, and about 8:00 PM forty-seven Utes arrived from Ignacio, Colorado.

The Navajos were sent to the south end to patrol that area and the Utes fell in with the ECW crew on building the fire trail to the North Rim. The trail was carried to a completion at noon Sunday, July 15, by working all night, with only enough time out for a hurried supper and breakfast. ...

Due to the location of the fire front it was too dangerous to put men down in the canyon during the night, but as soon as it was light Sunday morning a crew of twenty-four Park men, seventeen of them being Navajos, went to the fire front at the North Rim, where the flames seemed to be making the most advance and which was also the strategic point to control future advance. All through the morning of Sunday, July 15, the wind was quiet and everything seemed favorable to not have to back-fire along the great fire lane, but at 1:30 PM the wind changed into the north and came up sharp, throwing the flames across the small fire trail constructed by the early morning patrol, and the efforts of the

twenty-four men were, or should there have been ten times that many, inadequate, for all had to run for their lives as the flames advanced so rapidly. When the men arrived at the big fire lane and explained the situation it was decided best to back-fire immediately from the fire lane.

In the meantime several hundred fire fighters had arrived from Durango, Shiprock, Towaoc, Ignacio, and some from as far away as Fort Defiance and Fort Apache. Men were stationed about every thirty feet along the mile and half line, while others equipped with torches made from hats and a torn blanket saturated with oil, started down the line igniting the grass and brush along the west edge of the fire lane. By 7:30 PM the wind had died down and as the back-fire had been a success the crews were transported in relays to the fly camp for supper. The main part of the night's work was patrol duty and watching for sparks that might have jumped to the east side of the fire line.

Since there were now seemingly adequate fresh men on the fire line it was thought best to relieve the ECW and Park crews, many of whom had seen four days and nights of continuous service.

The weary firefighters received some much needed R&R, and finally on July 25 the fire was declared out and the area safe to leave. Some 4,500 acres had burned in both fires, nearly half within the park boundaries.

Because dense stands of piñon-juniper were a treasured trait of the park, CCC laborers were then brought back to the burned landscape to plant tens of thousands of seedling piñon and juniper trees in a largely fruitless attempt at reforestation. (They did not realize that piñon and juniper could not be replanted after fire the same way that Douglas fir and other tall conifers can be in more moist environments.) CCC laborers worked diligently to gently nestle construction projects within the park's woodlands and carefully replant trees and shrubs around new buildings, parking lots, and along road cuts.

Throughout the rest of the twentieth century, complete fire suppression continued to be the goal: every fire was fought under every circumstance. To complicate this goal, the second half of the twentieth century was as active with fire as the first half-century was inactive. Despite ever-improving firefighting technology and capability, major

During the 1930s, members of the CCC fought some tremendous fires in the park, and after the fires were out they did the lion's share of replanting the bare ground.

wildfires struck the park in 1959, 1972, 1989, 1996, 2000, 2002, and 2003. About 80 percent of the park's acreage has experienced fire since the national park was established. Of those fires, the most devastating were the Bircher and Pony Fires of 2000, which together burned more than 29,000 acres, just under 20,000 of them in the park.

The Bircher Fire began on July 20, 2000, at 1:30 P.M., when lightning struck the Bircher farm just east of Mesa Verde. With fearsome speed, the fire sped westward into the park, and in three days it had blown out of control. The fire raced unchecked for days, in an uninterrupted march to the west. Flames surrounded Park Point, the highest point on the mesa, and the historic fire lookout tower there was saved only by a wrapping of fire-resistant material.

At the peak of the Bircher Fire hundreds of firefighters struggled to contain the blaze, digging fire lines by

CLOCKWISE FROM TOP LEFT

Smoke from the Chapin #5 Fire in 1996 loomed over the Far View Visitor Center. Air tankers worked all day laying down a line of slurry in front of the visitor center and Far View Lodge in their successful attempt to save both structures.

You can almost see the pilot of this tanker as he flies low over the target area, maximizing the effect of the slurry drop.

Flames of the approaching fire front moved rapidly upcanyon and upslope during the peak burning period of mid- to late afternoon.

Exhaustion shows after a long day of fire fighting; active flames indicate another long day in store tomorrow for firefighters.

A smoke column from the Bircher Fire in 2000 approached 56,000 feet, according to the National Weather Service. A plume-dominated fire like this one creates its own weather, and the result is very erratic fire behavior.

Early in the Bircher Fire, one of the helicopters assigned to the incident borrowed water from a local landowner's pond to reduce time between drops on the fire.

CLOCKWISE FROM TOP LEFT

This picture clearly shows the success of a double-pronged approach in protecting the archaeological sites in the park. Thinning of trees around the sites combined with retardant drops along the edge of the thinned area saved this remarkable mesa-top site.

Morefield Campground as a flame front approaches. Firefighters' preparations paid off; the Campground sustained very little damage.

While there were hundreds of previously unrecorded archaeological sites uncovered by the Chapin #5 Fire, most were small rubble mounds like this one. No new Cliff Palaces emerged from the ashes.

An air tanker in mid-drop during the Chapin #5 Fire shows the magnitude of the fire and how small men and all their machines are against the onslaught.

Fortunately the heavy equipment in the foreground did not have to be used to defend structures during the Bircher Fire in 2000 in Morefield Campground.

Mop-up can be a dangerous time on a fire because of unstable, partially burned trees. Firefighters scouring the burn are looking for hot spots and falling trees. It is certainly the dirtiest time on a fire with all the ash—crews always return to camp at the end of the day black from head to toe.

hand because bulldozers would have harmed archaeological sites. Slurry bombers dropped hundreds of thousands of pounds of fire retardant from the air. Park visitors and personnel were evacuated hurriedly. Rangers looked back with tears in their eyes, and black bears took refuge in the rooms of Spruce Tree House.

The Bircher Fire was finally contained after nine days, but it was followed immediately on August 4 by a fire that started in Pony Canyon on the Ute Mountain Ute Reservation. Winds spread the Pony Fire onto Wetherill Mesa, where it scorched visitor facilities near Long House and Step House. It came within a mile of park headquarters and the research center where nearly 3 million artifacts are housed. Together the two fires burned slightly less than half the park—and in their intensity and magnitude rewrote the park's fire history.

An article in the July 25, 2000, *Denver Post* carried the headline, "Heart of Mesa Verde in grave danger." The reporter described the fear and immediate devastation of the Bircher Fire:

> A 5-day-old wildfire has devoured 22,000 acres of Mesa Verde, almost half the park, and it was threatening one of the world's greatest collections of antiquities Monday.
>
> The Bircher fire attacked more slowly Monday, growing by about 5,000 acres, but firefighters were as wary as ever. They said they could not predict where the fire would go next.
>
> "This tops the list of extreme fire behavior ever experienced," said Justin Dombrowski, spokesman for the command center. "This is awesome power. When you have 200-foot-length flames, you're not going to do anything to stop it."
>
> The plume of smoke has reached 50,000 feet high, fire analyst Mike Frary said. "It's one of those things you don't see often in a career."
>
> The fire has burned its way to within 4 miles of Balcony House and Cliff Palace. … It was closer to park headquarters and the research center on Chapin Mesa.
>
> The heart of the park was in grave danger of burning.

"This could happen. This could happen today or tomorrow," park archaeologist Linda Towle told employees at a Monday afternoon meeting. "That is the reality. … "

> In the wake of the nation's most confounding wildfire, the scene is blacker and bleaker than the dark side of the moon. On Mesa Verde's charred northern and eastern borders nothing is moving except smoke devils swirling in fits of wind and a dazed deer. Now only rare patches of grass cling to life in scorched earth. …
>
> Even if main park structures and the irreplaceable remnants of the ancient Puebloans are saved, much of the landscape is covered in ash. …

Mesa Verde's visitation was cut in half that summer. Surrounding communities, which sustained heavy economic losses, complained that the park service did not move fast enough to halt the fires' spread. An investigation noted some confusion during the transition of fire crews and mobilization of air support in the first days of the Bircher Fire, but concluded that agencies were not at fault for the fires' swift growth. The transition of fire crews and leadership teams is always the most dangerous time on a fire, with firefighter and public safety of greatest concern.

Fire has been a prominent feature of Mesa Verde's landscape for as long as records have been kept. Since the park's creation in 1906, lightning-caused fires have burned the oak, piñon, and juniper forests with regularity in the summer: the 1934 Wild Horse Mesa Fire fought by CCC crews; Morefield Canyon in 1959; Moccasin Mesa in 1972; Long Mesa in 1989; and the Chapin #5 Fire in 1996 that burned some 4,700 acres in the Far View area.

In the wake of the fires of the late 1990s and the summers of 2000 and 2002, the Burned Area Emergency Rehabilitation (BAER) team assessed damage and took steps to protect sites from erosion and exotic plants that tend to sprout up in the disturbed soils. Unlike most other forest types in the West, when Mesa Verde's piñon-juniper woodlands burn, they tend to go up either as single trees or all at once in a stand-replacing crown fire. The trees do not resprout and do not even begin to seed into the burned areas for a century or more. This can make way for nonnative species, though mountain shrublands of oak, mountain mahogany, and serviceberry, all native to the region, may also actively resprout immediately after fire. With a stand turnover time of only about 100 years, these species are far more fire adapted than the piñon-juniper.

Another side effect of the ground-baring fires is the revelation of more archaeological sites, most of them scatters of potsherds. Archaeologists are revisiting the burned areas to map and inventory all those sites. Biologists are also monitoring the effects on wildlife, whose food and shelter obviously were damaged. The park is evaluating further reduction of the "fuel load," the buildup of trees after a long period of suppression, to prevent such catastrophic fires. Several other studies have looked at fire and landscape recovery. One thing is certain—Mesa Verde has not seen the last of wildfire.

AIR QUALITY

In the mid-1960s and into the 1980s the modern world began to press in on Mesa Verde from above. Looming on the horizon, literally, was the specter of deterioration of the park's once pristine air quality. During those years a pair of coal-fired power plants had been built in stages due south of the park in New Mexico: the San Juan and Four Corners plants. In response, the park installed monitoring equipment on Chapin Mesa to measure air quality. With it, park staff record visibility, acid rain, and ozone. Data collected indicates that there has been significant deterioration of the park's air quality over the years. The natural resources division reported in 1998 that even though the park still enjoyed some of the cleanest air in the lower forty-eight states, "maximum visibility now is down to about 75 miles and still deteriorating."

Industrial development, including more natural gas production and coal-burning electric plants, as well as population increases, are the culprits. Like many other national parks, Mesa Verde no longer enjoys large buffers from development, making it more difficult for the park to retain a natural character. At just over 52,000 acres, Mesa Verde is not large enough to possess self-sustaining ecological processes. Actions that take place outside the park—growing towns and cities, agriculture, mining, oil and gas exploration, and many additional factors—have a profound effect on the natural resources inside the park. All of the natural elements that make Mesa Verde a haven from the modern, developed world, including the water quality and flow levels of the Mancos River, scenic views, dark night skies, natural sounds and quiet, and abundant wildlife and fish species, must be protected and defended.

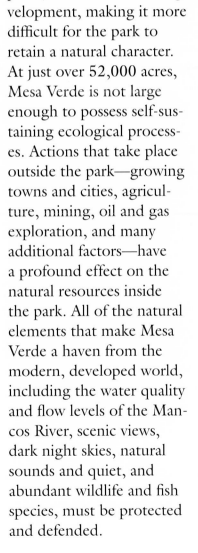

Charles Douglas works on an air quality monitoring device.

SUCCESS

Even with environmental pressures bearing down on Mesa Verde, the park has had wildlife success stories, thanks to help from the Colorado Division of Wildlife (CDOW). In 1990, CDOW successfully reestablished wild turkeys in the park after an introduced poultry disease wiped out the native turkeys. CDOW also successfully reestablished a herd of bighorn sheep at Mesa Verde in 1946, though the population has not been self-sustaining. Rocky Mountain elk numbers have increased to as many as 200 bulls and cows. How habitat changes from the recent spate of wildfires will affect these species is not known. One great success began in 2002, when CDOW helped rescue some of the last roundtail chub (a native fish) from the drying Mancos River and placed them into a captive breeding program. Starting in 2004, CDOW biologists have returned thousands of young chub to the river along with many adult bluehead and flannelmouth suckers.

LINKING THE PAST WITH THE FUTURE

The Ancestral Puebloans of Mesa Verde were irrevocably tied to the natural world. That essential connection between the prehistoric culture of Mesa Verde and its natural history is evident in archaeological excavations of food, clothing, tools, building materials, artwork, and other human possessions. Largely the same native flora and fauna existed in the prehistoric environment as we see today. Indirectly, this suggests that our climate is much the same as the climate at Mesa Verde a thousand years ago. The evolution of the Mesa Verde culture, found abundantly throughout the park, can only be fully understood within the context of the natural environment.

For the better part of a millennium, the Ancestral Puebloan people used and altered the natural world at Mesa Verde. They cut down forests, planted crops, hunted wildlife, and probably used fire to manipulate vegetation. Six centuries after their departure, nature had largely reclaimed the landscape. Then, in the early years of the twentieth century, modern civilization took up residence here, setting aside Mesa Verde as a living cultural museum and nature preserve. But in the century since—a relatively brief time—modern society has once again heavily taxed the limited natural bounty of the land, air, and water in and around the park. The Ancestral Puebloans found it necessary to leave Mesa Verde, some say because of excessive population, drought, deforestation, soil exhaustion, social strife, or a combination of these factors. We need to learn from these lessons so that the same results do not occur.

Most people see the natural resources of Mesa Verde as little more than scenery, a spectacular backdrop for the cliff dwellings. Yet although Mesa Verde was set aside for its cultural riches, the park's enabling legislation was amended in 1928 to reflect the need to preserve "from injury or spoilation … all timber, natural curiosities, or wonderful objects" and to protect "the animals and birds in the park." This reflects an earlier study by the National Park Service in 1916, which declared that " … our greatest national heritage is nature itself, which, when combined with great scenic beauty as it is in the national parks, becomes of unlimited value." In the twenty-first century, park administrators must protect the park's ecological health in the face of the modern world's rapid encroachment. Park managers have to be willing to extend the park's message, needs, and concerns far beyond the park boundaries into the communities and boardrooms where many of these problems originate. There are positive signs.

In the late 1990s, the Natural Resource Challenge was unveiled by the National Park Service to invigorate natural resource stewardship in the parks. Additionally, in recent years researchers from many different disciplines have found Mesa Verde to be a valuable outdoor laboratory in which to study nature and then publish the results. This new information can make a great difference in improving management direction.

Natural history is the other half of the Mesa Verde story. Appreciating and celebrating the park's wild side does not distract visitors from Mesa Verde's archaeology, it enhances and helps to explain it. Like every other national park, Mesa Verde's mission is multidimensional: " … to conserve the scenery and the natural and historic objects and the wild life therein … unimpaired for the enjoyment of future generations."

Yucca fiber was used to weave one of the most important articles of clothing to the Puebloans, the sandal. Shown is a sandal from the Basketmaker Period.

SANDSTONE AND SUNSHINE
An Essay by Ann Haymond Zwinger

At a few minutes of seven, imminent dawn shows as a string of cerise yarn stretched taut along the eastern quadrant of Mesa Verde, kept thin by an overcast sky that sits on it like a lid. The wind wheezes and shrieks, frets and frisks the rabbitbrush and sagebrush, and will sweep away the clouds. I grab a heavy jacket and head for breakfast and Cliff Palace.

I haven't seen Cliff Palace, the crown jewel of Mesa Verde, for years. That adds an edge to my anticipation that no weather can congeal—seeing it again with more-informed eyes, posing questions I didn't know enough to ask then, pondering the ingenuity of human solutions. One of those solutions—a yucca leaf—pokes me in the leg like a bayonet. These leaves answered a great many needs for the Ancestral Puebloans, primarily for weaving magnificent baskets, but also for making cordage, soap, sandals and booties, pot rests and pot mending, hairbrushes and paintbrushes, tump bands and fabric. The sharp tips, with fiber attached, served as needles for sewing. Women in prolonged labor once received a tea to ease the birth (presumably with dosage delicately balanced because its high concentration of saponin makes it highly toxic). Yucca soap from the roots is still used for ceremonial hair washing, and the fruits, peeled and raw, are still relished.

I rub a sprig of sagebrush between my fingers and sniff the evocative and quintessential perfume of the Southwest, yet another of the medicinal plants, rich in iron and vitamin C. Like most of Mesa Verde's plants, sagebrush is a perennial; the paucity of annuals marks just how difficult the growing season is here. Perennials, once established, are able to survive; those that must sprout from seed each year can't.

Our ranger guide arrives and leads ten of us downward through a sandstone slot. Across the canyon, the Long Mesa Fire of 2002 left a charred calling card along the edge of the cliff, a landscape traced in India ink with a spavined pen nib. When the Puebloans lived here, they cleared the canyon for firewood and construction and burned the woodlands to create open land for farming and rangeland for game animals, likely reducing the chance of catastrophic fires like those that have scorched the park in the last decade.

We enter the site via its south end, just as original excavator Jesse Walter Fewkes did, and the impact must have been even more dazzling for him than it is for me today. The whole splendid sunlit panoply of Cliff Palace stretches more than 400 feet before me. I've just looked at the "before" pictures in Fewkes's book when the site was a mammoth jumble of rubble and defiled by vandalism. In 1909 Fewkes did extensive reconstruction on the buildings, his aim "to repair completely this great ruin," a noble idea probably not carried out with today's sophisticated techniques. Fewkes admired the careful dressing of the stones, the clean right-angles, the care and skill of the original builders who constructed walls to lie parallel or perpendicular to the alcove floor's natural slope. We enter walking, just as the Ancestral Puebloans did, so that the full view of Cliff Palace opens, step by step.

Water hollowed out this huge alcove from Cliffhouse Sandstone, percolating through the porous sandstone layers until it met an impervious layer of shale. The shale forced water to gather and run laterally until it reached canyon walls where it broke out as seeps and springs. Freezing and thawing weakened the sandstone until it spalled off in great slabs and opened vast cavities which the Ancestral Puebloans utilized as living space for a century, A.D. 1200 to 1300.

Cliff Palace, crown jewel of Mesa Verde.

Cliffhouse Sandstone is the uppermost layer of the Mesaverde Group, a massive deposit of shoreline sediments laid down between 120 and 65 million years ago. It varies in color from warm beige, pocked with little depressions, to cold gray-white with traces of mauve and mustard and lavender, with ghosts of ivory and bone, intermingled muted colors telling stories of old Cretaceous seashores and seabeds. For me, this use of country rock imbues Cliff Palace with a special character; it is not superimposed upon the landscape, but because it's built of the same sandstone as its framing oval, it becomes of its landscape as well as in it. It unifies man's work with nature's work.

I, like so many others, can't help but wonder why the early Puebloans chose to build in these places so difficult of access, when they had essentially ignored them for eight centuries, occupying instead the mesa tops closer to the fields. Of the 4,500 dwellings in the park, only 600 were situated in alcoves, and the building of the cliff houses coincided with the last century of Mesa Verde occupation. As population expanded, a need to exploit new places to live, a possible need for defense, or greater protection from the elements, plus proximity to secure water supplies, have been suggested.

Tree-ring dates register that the first stones were laid here around 1200, beginning in the back left of the cave where a spring flowed. Construction proceeded right out to the drip line, room arrangement dictated by constricted space, creating a plan-as-you-go aggregation of rooms. This large complex took an astoundingly short twenty years to erect despite the time it must have taken to dress thousands of sandstone blocks for some 150 rooms and 23 kivas—its sheer size distinguishes Cliff Palace. Rectilinear blocks of sandstone joined by mortar with an ash binder, and juniper lintels, result in a harmony derived from a simple repetition of vertical and horizontal. The window and door placement reminds me of a Mondrian painting, balance and variety arranged within a stringent framework.

At one time, archaeologists speculate, half of the thirteenth-century population lived and worked here, and Cliff Palace was more likely a "community center" than a residential one. No campfire smoke blackens any putative "residential" rooms, which suggests these rooms may not have been used in cold weather. Recent studies of temperatures in roofed rooms such as kivas, both here and on the rims, document that they were the warmest places during severe winters. The traditional assumption that kivas were exclusively ceremonial chambers is being revised to suggest that kivas at times also served as communal living spaces.

The function of many rooms other than kivas is not decipherable; such undefined rooms appeared as the population increased and more people clustered into larger groups as they did at this time in the history of Mesa Verde. But I am looking at Cliff Palace through the scrim of Western art history, evaluating wall placement and construction techniques when, to the prehistoric eye, these were not the end points but merely extensions of the natural world about them. The space within, with its functions and ceremonial connotations, carried more meaning than the material walls.

Nearly all the occupants were gone from Mesa Verde by the early 1300s for various reasons: twenty-five years of the Great Drought of 1276–1299 and other anomalous weather factors; overpopulation, brought on by improved nutrition, that overstepped the carrying capacity of the land; perhaps social unrest or epidemics caused by crowding. The unfortunate concatenation combined to make life untenable here, leaving only gritty witness walls.

Two loop roads run along the mesa top, giving access to sites where Ancestral Puebloans lived before they built the cliff houses. The convenience of good roads to enhance

94

viewing has always been a primary aim of the park, beginning in 1906 when the first survey of the park was made; most of those routes are still in use today. The loop drive meanders along the edges of the mesa with stops at early pit houses and other sites that in many ways offered more practical living space than the cliff dwellings. People occupied the mesa top as early as A.D. 550, where the red loessial soil, blown in over eons, was fertile and retained water well. Unfettered space provided these mesa-top sites with a sequence of building plans over time, simpler and more straightforward than those of the cliff dwellings.

The roads also provide stunning views of inaccessible cliff dwellings in the opposite canyon walls. Across the canyon, diminished in scale by distance, is Oak Tree House, from here an abstract pattern of forms and shadows. A fringe of piñon-juniper woodland serrates the horizon, and pennants of desert varnish streak the overhang. Manganese and iron, both deposited by water and blown in as dust and fixed by bacterial action, create these distinctive caparisons on the rocks. Oak Tree House reminds me of the miniature Tuscan and Flemish villages painted in the background of devotional panels by Giotto or Dürer, grottos framing the backgrounds for Nativity scenes, or for St. Jerome and St. Anthony in the wilderness. To these painters the grotto personified protection from surrounding wildness, but never could they have conceived of such a city tucked into such a huge natural grotto.

I reach Sun Temple just at dusk. The builders sited it at the edge of a finger of the mesa, whence it looks into Cliff Canyon, with a view of a miniature Cliff Palace. Toward the end of the occupation period at Mesa Verde, different forms of ceremonial structures appeared. Here builders encased two kivas within two massive concentric D-shaped walls. They did not use traditional construction of single block–thick walls but built double walls of smaller blocks,

the gap between filled with rubble. Pecked dots or geometrics decorated individual blocks. Sun Temple possibly may have served as a "solar marker," as some archaeologists (arguably) think other structures in the Four Corners may have. But the Puebloans departed before they finished, leaving behind an imposing building placed with dramatic effect, a question with no answer.

Mesa Verde's focus is on its archaeological sites, not on hiking and backpacking in the backcountry. But there is a handsome hike to Petroglyph Point along the flank of Spruce Canyon. At noon, while sunshine gives hope of good weather, clouds soup up over the horizon, rain arrives and progresses quickly from intermittent showers to a sullen downpour. If you took a poll about weather in the Southwest, I suspect the consensus would paint it as bright and sunny: hard-edged with vast cloudless skies, the weatherman's definition of "severe clear." Which is largely true. But on this October day, it's all rain and fog, squish and drip.

Every overhang is a haven of dryness, and I don't miss a single one. Entering the first, I instantly feel its protectiveness and, in a flash, have insight into exactly what someone here 800 years ago must have felt: it's blessed dry in here! As quickly as it began, the rain stops, succeeded by a breath-holding silence. Not a leaf bends, not a needle flickers, not a footstep crunches, only the sacrilegious sound of pencil assaulting paper. I stop writing and absorb the impeccable stillness—no witless breeze, no sounds of leaf growing or drying or falling—steeping me in the simple silence of listening.

A gargantuan flashbulb explodes in the canyon. Four seconds later thunder rumbles like a giant's borborygmus. No wonder the Ancestral Puebloans were so aware of their environment—nothing existed between them and a distant thunder roll miles away and, likewise, between them and the sound of a piñon cone opening, nothing between them and a grain of sand falling out of the cliff face. An exquisite, healing silence we no longer easily find in our lives except in sequestered places like this.

The rain resumes, a delicate, wavering silver-bead curtain draped across the canyon. Back on the trail, rivulets swizzle down the path. I cross a rock-rib divide and now the rivulets run with me, a hand span wide. Lichens scab the sandstone, brightened by moisture emblazoning them with new colors: gray wakes up to powder blue or sage green, peppered with fruiting bodies, fat and fertile. These crustose minutiae dominate the lichen flora in Mesa Verde, occurring predominantly on Cliffhouse Sandstone, important in weathering the rock upon which they grow.

When I finally reach the petroglyphs, I shift my hood back so I can look upward. I shiver when the rain slithers down the front of my neck. Many medium- and small-sized figures crowd in a narrow band above my head. Some archaeologists suggest this is a "passage panel"; a modern Hopi interpretation identifies them as origin and migration symbols, as well as clan and spirit symbols represented by the bighorn sheep (the Mountain Sheep Clan) and two birds facing each other (the Parrot Clan).

One large and two smaller figures stretch their arms outward at shoulder height, bent at the elbows so that the hands are raised, palms forward: the pose of an orant, a praying figure that appears in figure representations from earliest times. The Hopi believe they are representations of Puebloan people, the raised arms showing they have nothing to hide.

The handprints must have been arduous to chip out with a rock hammer. There may be some kind of supernatural power associated with hands, or as individual marks they may have granted the carver some hoped-for immortality or emphasized the powers of a godlike figure. But no one knows for sure what was in the mind of the artist or what these figures meant to the viewer. To have spent such time and effort means to me that these artisans were not just doodling but creating figures of intense and fairly precise meaning, conveying universals and particulars imbued with portent, archetypical ideas whose power communicates without translation.

A short, steep climb up to the top of the mesa connects to the return path. The trail runs smoothly on an open sandstone apron with a view down across the canyon. Here, the landscape is in mourning, the ground black as ebony, shrubs like sticks of charcoal, needles still clinging to dismal trees: again the Long Mesa Fire's legacy. A mountain mahogany, giddy optimist, sprouts tiny bright green leaves on blackened twigs. Gray drifts of ash pattern the ground. Where the burn is total, trees and soil look as if seared by a dragon with incandescent breath that incinerated everything—tree, shrub, rock, lichen, grass, ground. On this unremitting blackness, meter-wide stripes of straw snake between ebony trees, placed to hinder erosion. Containment of the Long Fire came scarcely a week after it started, thanks to well-organized planning for just this eventuality by park personnel. Since 1996 fires, including Long Mesa, have burned almost half the park's acreage but touched none of the major sites. Archaeologists, accompanying fire crews to do "archaeology on the run," identified and marked many more sites uncovered by the flames. Fire is not a totally unmitigated disaster: it injects phosphorus and nitrogen into the soil, improves habitat for some snag-nesting birds, and the more-open woods benefit bighorn sheep (whose reintroduction is again under consideration).

Fire has *always* been a part of Mesa Verde. Small fires occur nearly every summer, the result of lightning strikes, and can be stopped fairly quickly. The combination of vegetation and climate—a heavy cover of piñon-juniper woodlands with highly flammable undergrowth, an average eighteen inches of precipitation a year or less, and frequent summer thunderstorms with plenty of Zeusian lightning—makes fire a constant concern. The remaining piñon-juniper woodlands at Mesa Verde are likely to be some of the oldest stands on the Colorado Plateau. Piñon and juniper trees have a very high mortality rate even in low-intensity fires. Unlike species such as ponderosa or lodgepole pines, the comparatively thin bark of the piñon and juniper trees does not resist fire. For those trees torched by the Long Mesa 2 Fire, it will be nearly 300 years before their replacements attain full height, and much longer still until the stand attains the same density.

Under the prehistoric land-use patterns, regular clearing out of dead trees for building, farming, and fuel—ironically resembling today's "mechanical fuel reduction"—probably kept fires down to manageable proportions. When Mesa Verde became a national park, it accepted federal government policy of "total fire control," where *all* fires were fought. A critical buildup of fuel resulted. From 1906 until 2003, about 70 percent of Mesa Verde burned; in the last twenty-five years, the number of fires has increased by twenty to twenty-five a year, including the large fires of 2000 and 2002. Clearly total fire control is not possible, and new policies will make changes.

The Petroglyph Point Trail ends at Spruce Tree House where the fire had begun to lick downslope until the wind spun around and turned it back. Chance, I suppose, but in this spiritual space it is easy to believe other forces were at work. In the damp, chilling air I feel murmurings and rustlings and chatterings of busy households, and that important obeisance needs to be made. The Ancestral Puebloan pantheon contained spirits in touch with rainstorms and weather, hunting and harvests, fertility and prosperity, a close connection to the natural world. I honor that particular courtesy and deep respect that has always characterized people living close to the earth.

In the late afternoon as I drive northward, the thousand-foot rise of Chapin Mesa turns rain to snow. A late sun draws long streaks of pale sunshine on distant blue-tan East Rim. Above it the sky remains icy pale, hung with flotillas of powder-blue cumulus clouds, totally still. Here, snow sifts down from an amorphous foggy cloud just above me, infused with pink by a setting sun: two weathers, like two trains passing in the night, a visual Doppler effect at the end of a marvelous day.

The next morning as I leave, I discover inches of snow on the ground and more coming down by the boxful. Snow caps each rabbitbrush seed head, outlines wildly interwoven scrub oak branches. This pristine covering envelops the gone-down of summer, the fast-fade of fall, the cold sibilant whisper of winter, the devout desire for spring. Mesa Verde huddles into itself. Cold silence hangs in the dwellings and curtains the doorways, centuries on hold. It is not yet time for Sun to leave his Winter House and start northward to spring.

⊕ ANN HAYMOND ZWINGER is an award-winning natural history writer, author of more than a dozen books and many magazine essays. Her book *Run, River, Run* won the John Burroughs Medal, and *Land Above the Trees* was nominated for a National Book Award. The ORION Society gave her the John Hay Award for "achievement in writing, conservation, and education." Zwinger is also an accomplished artist. She makes her home in Colorado Springs with her husband, Herman Zwinger, but also spends a "large amount of time happily working in faraway places with strange-sounding names."

CHAPTER 7

SEEING MESA VERDE: INSPIRATION FOR ARTISTS AND WRITERS

I n 1925 photographer Laura Gilpin wrote of Mesa Verde, "There is something infinitely appealing in this land." That sentiment is recognized by even the most casual visitor, but is expressed most eloquently by the photographers, writers, and artists who have been inspired by this place. Though interpretations of Mesa Verde are sometimes romanticized or lack cultural sensitivies, artistic reactions to the park over the last century provide a fascinating look at how we see the past—whether it be through a lens, on paper, or on canvas.

A MESA HUNG WITH VILLAGES: WILLA CATHER

Among the thousand or so people who made the trek to the park in 1915 was author Willa Cather and companion Edith Lewis. They took the train from Denver to Mancos, then traveled to Mesa Verde. Cather likely could have heard or read about Mesa Verde when she was growing up in Red Cloud, Nebraska, and would later obviously be influenced by Gustaf Nordenskiöld's landmark Mesa Verde publication and by Jesse Walter Fewkes, who was working in the park at the time of her visit.

This was Cather's second trip to the Southwest (she had traveled to northern Arizona in 1912 to visit her brother). The Mesa Verde visit inspired an essay that was published as a newspaper story in the January 31, 1916, *Denver Times.* The essay would become grist for her 1925 novel, *The Professor's House*, whose main character, Tom Outland, was based on Richard Wetherill. Many other similarities to Mesa Verde appear in the novel, only thinly veiled by literary license.

In her 1916 essay, Cather describes the trip on the Denver & Rio Grande Railroad, nicknamed "the Whiplash" as it swung through the mountains southwest of Denver. They spent the night in Durango, then rode the Rio Grande Southern into Mancos. From that little burg, of which she became most fond, Cather remarked on the view of the "darkish purple" mass of Mesa Verde. During their week of exploring in Mesa Verde, Cather and Lewis, even with a guide, had gotten lost. While the guide went for help, the two women watched sunset and moonrise in a lonely canyon deep in the park. Within twenty-four hours, they were rescued. Though Cather did not make a large issue of the experience, local newspaper headlines rendered the ordeal with high drama.

For Willa Cather, it was all part of the moving emotional

Willa Cather at Mesa Verde, 1915

OPPOSITE: *Mesa Verde's star-filled night skies inspired artist D.J. Webb's digital illustration* The Mystique of Mesa Verde.

experience she had at Mesa Verde. This excerpt from her 1916 essay reveals that reaction:

> [The] ruins [of Mesa Verde] are the highest achievement of stone-age man—preserved in bright, dry sunshine, like a fly in amber—sheltered by great cañon walls and hidden away in a difficult mesa into which no one had ever found a trail. When Wetherill rode in after his cattle no later civilization blurred the outlines there. Life had been extinct upon the mesa since the days of the Cliff Dwellers. Not only their buildings, but their pottery, linen cloth, feather cloth, sandals, stone and bone tools, dried pumpkins, corn and onions, remained as they had been left. There were even a few well-preserved mummies—not many, for the cliff dwellers cremated their dead.
>
> Altho only three groups of buildings have been excavated and made easily accessible to travelers, there are ruins everywhere—perched about like swallows' nests. The whole mesa, indeed, is one vast ruin. Eight hundred years ago the mesa was hung with villages, as the hills above Amalfi are today. There must have been about 10,000 people living there. The villages were all built back in these gracious natural arches in the cliffs; with such an outlook, such a setting as men have never found for their dwellings anywhere else in the world. The architecture is like that of most southern countries—of Palestine, northern Africa, southern Spain—absolutely harmonious with its site and setting. On the way from New York to the Montezuma valley one goes thru hundreds of ugly little American towns, but when you once reach the mesa, all that is behind you. The stone villages in the cliff arches are a successful evasion of ugliness—perhaps an indolent evasion. Color, simplicity, space, an absence of clutter, the houses of the Pueblo Indians today and of their ancestors on the Mesa Verde are a reproach to the messiness in which we live.
>
> Everything in the cliff dweller villages points to a tempered, settled, ritualistic life, where generations went on gravely and reverently repeating the past, rather than battling for anything new. Their lives were so full of ritual and symbolism that all their common actions were ceremonial—planting, harvesting, hunting, feasting, fasting. The great drama of the weather and the seasons occupied their minds a good deal, and they seem to have ordered their behavior according to the moon and sun and stars. The windows in the towers were arranged with regard for astronomical observations. Their strong habitations, their settled mode of living, their satisfying ritual, seem to have made this people conservative and aristocratic. The most plausible theory as to their extinction is that the dwellers on the Mesa Verde were routed and driven out by their vulgar, pushing neighbors of the plains, who were less comfortable, less satisfied, and consequently more energetic. …
>
> Dr. Johnson declared that man is an historical animal. Certainly it is the human record, however slight, that stirs us most deeply, and a country without such a record is dumb, no matter how beautiful. The Mesa Verde is not, as many people think, an inconveniently situated museum. It is the story of an early race, of the social and religious life of a people indigenous to that soil and to its rocky splendors. It is the human expression of that land of sharp contours, brutal contrasts, glorious color and blinding light. The human consciousness, as we know it today, dwelt there, and a feeling for beauty and order was certainly not absent. There are in those stone villages no suggestions revolting to our sensibilities. No sinister ideas lurk in the sun-drenched ruins hung among the crags. One has only to go down into Hopiland to find the same life going on today on other mesa tops; houses like these, kivas like these, ceremonial and religious implements like these—every detail preserved with the utmost fidelity. When you see those ancient, pyramidal pueblos once more brought nearer by the sunset light that beats on them like gold-beaters' hammers, when the aromatic piñon smoke begins to curl up in the still air and the boys bring in the cattle and the old Indians come out in their white burnouses and take their accustomed grave positions upon the housetops, you begin to feel that custom, ritual, integrity of tradition have a reality that goes deeper than the bustling business of the world.

THE ARCHITECTURE OF MARY COLTER

In 1902 a young architect took a summer job with the Fred Harvey Company. Mary Colter's work on the Indian Building at the Alvarado Hotel in Albuquerque launched a long and impressive career with the Harvey Company and Santa Fe Railroad.

Born in 1869 in Pittsburgh, the daughter of Irish immigrant parents, Mary Colter grew up in Saint Paul, Minnesota. Soon after graduating from the California School of Design in San Francisco, she landed the job that would define her life.

Colter's work with the Harvey Company, and its involvement with developing tourism in national parks, gave her the opportunity to travel widely in the Southwest. Her fascination with the region's Native American and Hispanic cultures was expressed in her building designs, which almost always incorporated rough-hewn local rock and wood. Interiors contained carefully detailed furniture and artwork by native people.

A long time friend of Mesa Verde's superintendent Jesse Nusbaum, Colter came to the park in the early 1930s. The elegant towers in some of the cliff dwellings inspired the design of her famed Watchtower at Desert View on the south rim of the Grand Canyon.

After forty-six years with the Harvey Company, Colter retired. Selling her home in California and moving to Santa Fe, she had to decide what to do with her large personal collection of Native American arts and crafts. She had already offered her jewelry to Mesa Verde, and in 1947 wrote to Don Watson at the park saying she favored the Mesa Verde museum as the repository for her Pueblo pottery and basketry. The park accepted the gifts and still displays a selection of them at the Far View Visitor Center.

Mary Elizabeth Jane Colter died in 1958, at age eighty-eight.

GHOST CITIES HIGH IN THE CLIFFS:
LOUIS L'AMOUR

In 1987, prolific western novelist Louis L'Amour published *Haunted Mesa*, one of nearly 120 books he wrote, with sales exceeding more than 260 million copies. Louis L'Amour lived and wrote for many years outside Durango, Colorado. He died in 1988, and his wife, Kathy, still lives part of the year in Colorado.

Haunted Mesa, a *New York Times* bestseller, has been called science, or fantasy, fiction. The action takes place in the vast wilderness just west of Mesa Verde, in southeast Utah. It revolves around the search for a wealthy, reclusive man, Erik Hokart, who went into the remote mesa and canyon country to build a home but turned up missing. His friend Mike Raglan is caught up in the search in a land where, as an old cowboy once told him, "there's canyons no man has seen the end of, nor ever will, either, unless they get through to the Other Side." Entwined in the story is this netherworld of the "Other Side," gained through a kiva, where people lived who had ties to the Ancestral Puebloans of the Four Corners.

In Haunted Mesa, *author Louis L'Amour used Mesa Verde and the Four Corners as his setting.*

Though this western mystery contains all the key elements—cowboys, Indians, and lost gold, with all the embellishments a fiction writer is allowed—L'Amour still chose to sneak in a few facts about Mesa Verde and the Ancestral Puebloans. Waking up one morning in a motel room in Monticello, Utah, Mike Raglan muses about European explorers who might have first "discovered" the dwellings tucked into the sandstone alcoves:

Seven hundred years ago all this country around, but mostly to the south, had been inhabited by those whom the Navajo called the Anasazi. This had been their land, its true length and breadth not yet established, nor the limits of its culture. Yet much was known of them.

Father Escalante had come this way seeking a route from Santa Fe to Monterey, California, in 1776. Father Garces, that intrepid adventurer in a cassock, had come up from the south, exploring a wild and lonely land, only to turn back. Who first had seen the cliff dwellings was without doubt one of those unknown hunters or prospectors who found almost everything before the official discoverers came on the scene.

W. H. Jackson, photographer for the U.S. Geological and Geographical Survey, was guided into the area by John Moss, who told him of the ruins and, when asked, indicated they could be found. Moss is sometimes represented as a mere miner. He was much more than that. He was a man who, leading a party of prospectors into Indian country, had no trouble with Indians. He met them, smoked with them, ate with them, and established a relationship that endured. No matter that others had trouble with the Utes, Moss did not. He had welded a friendship that was to last. ... Undoubtedly the Utes had told him of ghost cities high in the cliffs, and he was a man who would have been interested. Jackson, following the directions of Moss, visited at least one of the ruins. At the time no one had any appreciation of their size or extent. It remained for the explorations of the Wetherills to demonstrate that.

Jackson had gone into the sites in 1874, and others followed, guided by the Wetherills.

The cliff dwellings had been strongholds, but the people

were vulnerable when working in their fields. Invading Indians from the North, perhaps the Ute and the Navajo, had stolen their grain and killed many of their people. Nor had the cliff dwellings themselves been secure. The first white men to visit found the bones of the dead scattered about, pitiful evidence of what had taken place. …

The Anasazi themselves had come to the country from elsewhere and settled first on the mesa tops, where the ruins still remained, many of them hidden, however, by brush, trees, and grass. No matter what other reasons have been given, it seems obvious they would not have abandoned their mesa-top homes for the great caves without reason. Only a few of the cliff dwellings had springs, and water as well as food and fuel had to be carried into the cliff dwellings at great expenditure of labor.

CHAPIN MESA MUSEUM MURALS: TONITA PEÑA

One of Jesse Nusbaum's major accomplishments at Mesa Verde was initiating the Chapin Mesa Archaeological Museum. Construction on the first four rooms of the building began in 1923, and it was expanded over the years.

Exhibited in the auditorium there are six large murals created by artists from the Santa Fe Indian School. The school gave them to the park in 1935. Among the artists was Tonita Peña of San Ildefonso Pueblo, who painted this traditional scene of women, entitled *Making Piki*, 8¾ feet by 5⅝ feet in dimension.

Making Piki, by Tonita Peña, is one of six murals in the Chapin Mesa Archeological Museum.

COMING HOME:
LAURA GILPIN

Another famous artist, photographer Laura Gilpin, visited Mesa Verde in 1924 and 1925. She concluded "There is something infinitely appealing in this land," and part of that appeal for her was the human antiquity.

Born outside Colorado Springs in 1891, Laura Gilpin spent only a brief time studying photography in New York before returning to her beloved western homeland. She opened a commercial studio in Colorado Springs and made a name for herself as a landscape photographer in the 1920s in a field then dominated by men. Her chosen medium was black-and-white eight-by-ten-inch platinum prints. In her work, Gilpin strove to go beyond mere documentation, often using a soft-focus technique to capture the emotion of a scene.

After her first two visits to Mesa Verde, in 1927 a collection of her images was published in a book entitled *The Mesa Verde National Park: Reproductions from a Series of Photographs by Laura Gilpin*. She was primarily interested in how environment influenced human endeavor, how the spirit of place shaped cultures. To enhance that perspective, Gilpin sometimes posed Native American models in her scenes.

Her affection for her home country, especially southwest Colorado and northern New Mexico, resonated in her photos. Laura Gilpin continued to photograph and to travel the wide open spaces of the West until her death, in 1979, at age eighty-eight.

Colorado photographer Laura Gilpin was among those artists whose creative instincts were sparked by Mesa Verde.

OPPOSITE: *Two of Gilpin's photographs using Native American models at Mesa Verde*

THE COOKING JAR

THE HOUSE OF THE CLIFF DWELLER

Thomas McKee at work in the late 1800s with his eight-by-ten view camera, exposing glass plates. Imagine the challenge of transporting this equipment into and out of the rugged Mesa Verde terrain.

A MESA VERDE PORTFOLIO

Ever since William Henry Jackson captured the first image of Mesa Verde on film, photographers have continued to record their visual impressions of the park's stunning stone structures set in an incomparable landscape. They are captivated by the exquisite composition and form of the dwellings set so perfectly under alcoves or amid the forest. And, of course, for all photographers, it is the special quality of light that they seek. At Mesa Verde the luminous reflective light and the clarity of the air prove irresistible.

The following thirteen pages comprise a portfolio of photographs spanning more than 100 years. The diversity of images speaks to the photographer's individual response to this very special place.

Thomas McKee
Spring House, 1896

William Henry Jackson
Cliff Palace, 1896

Ansel Hall
Cliff Palace, 1947

Laurence Parent
Cedar Tree Tower, 1994

Steve Mulligan
Pipe Shrine House and Far View House, 2001

Claus Mroczynski
Reconstructed Pithouse, 2005

David Muench
Mug House, 1985

Adrial Heisey
Mesa Verde National Park Headquarters, 2005

Tom Bean
Pipe Shrine House, 1998

George H. H. Huey
Kodak House, 2002

116

Willard Clay
Square Tower House, 2001

Larry Ulrich
Mesa Verde Spring, 1995

EPILOGUE
An Essay by Duane A. Smith

W hat's past," Will Shakespeare opined in *The Tempest*, "is prologue." The bard might have been speaking about the saga of Mesa Verde National Park had he been in a position to do so. A little over a century later that fiery American patriot Patrick Henry explained further: "I have but one lamp by which my feet are guided, and that is the lamp of experience. I know no way of judging of the future but by the past." Those lessons of the past echo down through the decades and still shape visitors' impressions, experiences, and enjoyment during their visit to the park.

For the future of Mesa Verde and its heritage, let us hope that we have learned from the past. Starting with the reasons for abandonment by the Puebloan people, through the women's fight to create the park, to the crowds of the twenty-first century, lessons cry to be learned. Will we learn them or will future generations look back at us in amazement? That is the haunting question of a new century and a new millennium.

The Ancestral Puebloans were long gone by the time a coalition of women pressured and worked to achieve park status for the archaeological sites tucked in and about the canyons of the Mesa Verde. Conservationist and reformer President Theodore Roosevelt was more than willing in 1906 to add another national park to the country's growing list. Mesa Verde, however, proved different from its forebears and contemporaries—it preserved for future generations a cultural heritage, not solely a scenic gem. The federal government had already set the precedent for preserving an archaeological site at Arizona's Casa Grande, which became a national monument in 1889.

The group of women involved at Mesa Verde—the Colorado Cliff Dwellings Association—debated whether this park should be a state or federal one. The latter designation won, in a decision that, unfortunately, divisively split the group at the moment of victory. More than any one event, that decision shaped the future of Mesa Verde. Nothing else would be more significant. It would be Washington, D.C., that shaped the park's evolution. From minor issues to major controversies, the federal government would chart the course and guide developments.

From the nation's capital, the federal government nurtured into life the bare-bones promise on a piece of paper, a dream of dedicated women who determinedly spent a decade fighting to save what they considered a national treasure. In creating rules and regulations, appointing and hiring employees, and conducting park business, the government's hand was not always sure and steady, and sometimes it was not without the disappointments and strong feelings of local people.

Mesa Verde National Park begot fascinating and significant impacts upon a variety of matters and people. Most of the time, the limits of the park defined the extent of those impacts, yet sometimes they reached well beyond those artificial boundaries.

Nearby businessmen and -women expected much from the park's presence, but they did not always receive the bountiful blessings they anticipated. Over the years, there has been a love-hate attitude about Washington's involvement in the region. Nothing unusual in that—it was, is, and, no doubt, will be for decades to come a concern of most westerners. Mesa Verde offered the possibility of an economic bonanza for an often-depressed portion of southwestern Colorado. The park fulfilled that role, while at the same time failing to match expectations. It would be a while before the hordes of visitors, and their cherished dollars, would descend on local communities and businesses.

Colorado writer Eugene Parsons predicted a change would occur: "Hitherto Westerners have been too busy making a living and getting rich to bother their heads much about cliff dwellings and cave homes, but the time will come when men and women will feel a curiosity to know something of the prehistoric past of the Southwest." He was right. Still, no one could imagine what an impact the curiosity would have on the whole country and the world or predict the number of visitors that would eventually arrive.

Meanwhile, the act creating the park also created jealousies. The towns of Mancos, Cortez, and Durango squared off to lay claim to the title of gateway. Isolated, railroadless Cortez did not have a chance initially, as Mancos gained the early advantage. It secured the park headquarters and claimed the nearest railroad station to Mesa Verde. That advantage did not deter Durango—a "five-cent beer berg" as it was called by its little rival. Durango uproariously promoted itself, including publishing a map with the town and the park nearly side by side, and Mancos nowhere to be seen!

Despite Durango's proclivities, author Willa Cather enjoyed her weeklong summer stay in Mancos in 1915, a village and its inhabitants she charmingly described. "Before you know it you are staying on in Mancos because you like the people. The streets are lined with trees, the yards are a riot of giant sage and Indian paint brush, shaded with cedars; the wheat fields are a veritable cloth of gold and the whole town is buried in sweet clover." Mancos's moment of fame faded. Western urban rivalries tended to be cutthroat propositions, and Mancos never regained its early status.

The coming of the automobile and moving the headquarters into the park doomed Mancos's hopes. Durango's more numerous attractions and larger population surpassed its rival by the mid-1920s. Durango stood unchallenged in that position, until the post–World War II federal highway construction program finally tied Cortez into Flagstaff, Arizona, and southern California. Cortez's challenge briefly unnerved Durangoans, though realistically they had attained too much of a head start. Still, the nearly century-old rivalry persists, though a bit more subtly at the opening of the twenty-first century.

The "Mesa Verde Wonderland," as Cather idolized it, did not ebb, however. Yet in that "wonderland" loomed dilemmas. Having created the park, the federal government could not seem to please everybody—sometimes hardly anybody. The complaints ran the gamut. Criticism started with the original hiring of a superintendent and rangers in 1906–1907. Being political appointments in those days, their selection upset one party or the other. Mancos livery stable operators opposed opening the park to automobiles in 1914, while visitors complained the roads were so poor that they could not drive their cars into the park. Others objected to appointing archaeologist Jesse Nusbaum as superintendent in 1921, preferring to leave Mesa Verde as one of the region's best political plums. Realizing full well the implications, Mancos residents feared Nusbaum's act of moving the headquarters into the park. Park concessionaires complained about the government offering free, or cheap, camping locations. Federal and local trials and tribulations continued into the latter part of the century, with huge mud slides in 1979 that closed the park entrance road and immense fires in the summer of 2000 that devastated Mancos's and Cortez's economies and hurt even more-secure Durango. Again, controversy swirled around the fast-moving fires—what could, or should, have been done earlier to prevent such a disaster?

The park has also had its share of transportation problems. Mesa Verde has always been isolated, a major reason why it was not "discovered" and why it was vandalized long before its "discoverers," the Wetherills, arrived in the 1880s. Located far from any major urban center or accessible main travel routes (even the interstate highways are hours away today), Mesa Verde has always had to be a defined destination point, not a stop-off on a drive-by whim.

Early visitors found themselves mounted on horses traveling over rough trails on a one-day trip into the park. Not until 1923 was the infamous Knife Edge Road opened, which skirted the west side of Point Lookout. Without exaggeration, it was called "one of the most spectacular drives in America." A generation of tourists called it by other names, many of them not so complimentary. With a thousand-foot steep slope on one side and a cliff on the other, it in turn terrified, thrilled, challenged, and awed travelers. Prone to mud and rock slides, as well as sloughing downward, the road was abandoned in 1957.

Isolated Mesa Verde found its visitation in the hundreds and low thousands until the completion of the road over Wolf Creek Pass in the mountains to the east in 1916, which served to double the number of visitors to the park within a year. The eventual development of a better road system in Colorado and neighboring states, followed by the interstate system, stimulated more visitation here, and in all national parks for that matter. The fallout devastated the livery stable operators and hurt the concessionaires. A 1919 park service report stated that more than half the motorists toted their own camping equipment and had no need of lodging.

Superintendent Jesse Nusbaum quickly warned his superiors about traffic congestion and overcrowding. The park was already being loved to death, and automobiles only made it more accessible. Nusbaum reported the number of cars in the park each year jumped nearly eight times, to almost 5,000 by the end of the 1920s. Considering the condition of Colorado and New Mexico roads, this was an amazing increase. The specter of driving the road into Mesa Verde with the hair-raising "knife edge" section stopped some visitors, while others hired off-duty rangers to drive their cars over it. "The roads are perfectly safe and sane," observed 1927 park regulations: the driver "who does not care for his car and heed warnings is not."

The Rio Grande Southern and its controlling parent, the Denver & Rio Grande Railroad, had done much to promote Mesa Verde since the 1890s and had been the primary way to reach the park. But with the increasing popularity of the automobile, the number of tourists riding the train dwindled to a scattered few by the time of World War II. Railroads everywhere had fallen victim to Americans' love affair with their automobiles. The task then fell to the park itself, local towns, and automobile clubs to promote the park, and to bring people to it. For a brief time, Colorado's "baby" airline, Frontier, stepped into the void, but then it fell victim to the intense airline competition of the 1970s and the 1980s. For a time, the airline, like the railroad, became part of Mesa Verde's past, though in recent years it has made its way back.

It might seem like an oxymoron that both isolation and overcrowding confronted the park at the same time, nevertheless, they always have. The problems are timeless, and through the twenty-first century park officials and visitors will confront them just as people did a century ago.

Since the earliest days of Mesa Verde National Park, the quality of the visit has concerned superintendents and staff. Various approaches have been tried through the years—the creation of the museum, automobile caravans (1920s), public accommodations, opening Wetherill Mesa (1970s), self-guided tours, campfire talks, and limited "ticketed" tours to a few of the most popular sites. The "milling humanity" exceeded 100,000 in the month of July 1965. One ranger described that summer at Cliff Palace: "scuffling feet, wails of crying kids, the rangers' voices; bedlam is the rule of the day all summer long." The move of most accommodations from around the museum and park headquarters to the Far View complex a couple of years later helped ease some congestion but still could not really keep pace with the park's growing popularity.

Another seemingly mundane matter, water, was a pressing concern for the park. In the West, any kind of human habitation has always depended on a supply of it. The early Mesa Verdeans well knew that fact. The growing scarcity of water may have been one reason for their departure from the region. Few springs dot the mesa and canyons, creating a water shortage for visitors. The Colorado Cliff Dwellings Association initially confronted the problem and had some wells dug. The first superintendent, Hans Randolph, had a dam built at the head of Spruce Tree Canyon and dug cisterns to catch and store water for animals and tourists. Jesse Nusbaum improved upon those and added a covered one-acre catchment, which was connected to tanks to catch, filter, and store rainwater. Visitors' demands still exceeded supply. By 1930, the forecast of acute water shortages forced the planning process to begin all over again. To resolve the problem, water eventually had to be brought in from the La Plata Mountains through a thirty-mile pipeline finished in 1950. The enjoyment of the park and its treasures depends upon having an adequate water supply and is the key to any future development.

Mesa Verde has always brandished mysteries—why did the Puebloans move into the cliffs and why did they leave the region? The first visitors speculated that they might have been Aztecs driven north by the Spanish—hence the names Cortez and Montezuma County. As archaeologists have refined and improved their methods and skills of interpreting the past, we continue to gain a better understanding of who these people were. Sites are also being preserved for the future when new approaches may open unimagined vistas. Native Americans themselves, with long ties to Mesa Verde, are providing a different perspective.

Interpretations are not helped by vandalism, which has been around longer than the park itself. Will it ever stop? Not so long as there is a market for relics. People want souvenirs, and pothunters enjoy the excitement of the search and find. Nor is this a problem solely for park rangers. Despite federal laws, destruction of archaeological sites continues throughout the Four Corner states. Each time a bit of history and heritage is lost, never to be totally retrieved.

Unintentional destruction happens too. The large number of visitors tramping through the sites threatens to damage the fragile things they came to see. A continuing stabilization "war" has been conducted since the first months of the park's establishment. Recently this has taken on new meaning with air pollution and other environmental threats. Who can say what the future may bring? Undoubtedly, it will get worse before it gets better. The fight of the park's founding women to prevent vandalism and the possible destruction of Mesa Verde sites is one their descendants must not let falter.

Shakespeare was right, what's past is but a prologue. Mesa Verde, now a World Cultural Heritage Site, faces some of the same challenges that these women did in trying to save it. Every superintendent has worked hard with the same trials.

Yet "gloom, despair, and agony" is not the heritage that

results from all these issues. Rather optimism, understanding, appreciation, and concern more than counterbalance such negativism. There is a challenge in preserving Mesa Verde, a challenge that each generation has to accept. Each of us is a steward of this fantastic treasure. We owe that to those who came before and "fought the good fight."

In the words of Theodore Roosevelt, "far better it is to dare mighty things, to win glorious triumphs, even though checkered by failure, than to take rank with those poor spirits who neither enjoy much nor suffer much. ..." The challenges are great, the opportunities even greater.

⊕ DUANE A. SMITH received his doctorate from the University of Colorado in 1964, and since that time has been professor of history and southwest studies at Fort Lewis College in Durango, Colorado. His major areas of research and writing include western history, with an emphasis on mining and Colorado history. Smith is the author of *Mesa Verde National Park: Shadows of the Centuries.* He served as historical consultant for this book.

APPENDIX

SUPERINTENDENTS OF MESA VERDE NATIONAL PARK

William D. Leonard
Acting Superintendent
1906 to 1907

•

Charles F. Werner
Acting Superintendent
1907

•

Hans M. Randolph
Superintendent
1907 to 1911

•

F. B. Linnen
Acting Superintendent
1911

•

Richard Wright
Acting Superintendent
1911

•

Samuel Shoemaker
Superintendent
1911 to 1913

•

Thomas Rickner
Superintendent
1913 to 1921

•

Jesse L. Nusbaum
Superintendent
1921 to 1931

C. Marshall Finnan
Superintendent
1931 to 1933

•

Ernest P. Leavitt
Superintendent
1933 to 1935

•

Paul R. Franke
Acting Superintendent
1935

•

Jesse L. Nusbaum
Superintendent
1936 to 1937

•

Paul R. Franke
Superintendent
1939 to 1940

•

John S. McLaughlin,
Superintendent
1940 to 1942

•

Jesse L. Nusbaum
Acting Superintendent
1942 to 1946

•

John S. McLaughlin
Superintendent
1946

W. Ward Yesger
Acting Superintendent
1946

•

Robert H. Rose
Superintendent
1946 to 1952

•

Oscar W. Carlson
Superintendent
1952 to 1958

•

Chester A. Thomas
Superintendent
1958 to 1966

•

Meredith M. Guillet
Superintendent
1966 to 1972

•

Ronald R. Switzer
Superintendent
1972 to 1979

•

Robert C. Heyder
Superintendent
1979 to 1994

•

Larry T. Wiese
Superintendent
1994 to present

PERMISSIONS AND CREDITS

Copyrights on individual works published in this book are held by the artist or lending institution and may not be reproduced without their permission.

PERMISSIONS

Domínguez-Escalante translation—From the Spanish by Fray Angelico Chavez in *The Dominguez-Escalante Journal, Their Expedition Through Colorado, Utah, Arizona, and New Mexico in 1776*, edited by Ted J. Warner, University of Utah Press, 1995. The small site the fathers described may be what is now called Escalante Ruin, on a hilltop above the Anasazi Heritage Center north of Mesa Verde near Dolores, Colorado.

Kathleen Fiero, stabilization crew, from *Plateau Journal: Land and Peoples of the Colorado Plateau*, 2001 Spring/Summer issue, Museum of Northern Arizona, used by permission.

Excerpts by Douglas Osborne, *National Geographic* magazine, and Evan Connell, *National Geographic Traveler* magazine, used by permission, National Geographic Image Collection.

Willa Cather essay, used by permission of Charles Cather, Trustee.

Louis L'Amour excerpt, from *Haunted Mesa*, by Louis L'Amour, c 1987 by Louis L'Amour. Used by permission of Bantam Books, a division of Random House. L'Amour dedicated this book to Gilbert and Charlotte Wenger.

David Roberts excerpt, from "A Social Divide Written in Stone," *Smithsonian* magazine, February 1999, used by permission of author.

Denver Post editorial, used by permission of *Denver Post*, Denver, Colorado.

PHOTOGRAPHY CREDITS

Kay Barnett: p.45; Tom Bean: p. 65, 115; Fred Blackburn: p.45 (inset); Chicago Historical Society Archives: p. 13 (left); Willard Clay: p. 118; Colorado Historical Society: p. vi (bottom), xii, 11, 12, 14 (document), 22, 24, 26, 29, 33 (photo), 35, 36, 38, 49, 56, 57 (all), 59, 62, 64, 68 (bottom center), 70-71 (all), 108; Denver Public Library, Western History Department: p. i, xi, 31, 50 (call box), 51, 52 (both), 53 (both), 68 (left top and bottom, top right); *Durango Herald*: p. 28; Larry and Nancy Eifert: p. vii (painting), 78; Grand Canyon National Park Museum Collection: p. 101 (inset); Adriel Heisey: p. 6, 114; George H. H. Huey:p. v, vi (pot), ix, 4, 30, 48, 72, 82, 91, 92, 116-117; Mesa Verde Museum Association: p. 58 (inset); Mesa Verde National Park Collection: p. vi (newspaper clipping), x, 10, 13 (right), 14, 15, 16, 17, 18-19, 23, 27, 33 (report and detail), 34, 37, 39, 40-41, 43, 46, 47, 50 (stickers), 54 (photo), 55, 58, 60, 61 (bottom left), 63, 66 (photo), 67, 68 (bottom right), 73, 75, 77 (all), 80, 81, 84 (all), 85, 89, 102, 103, 104-105, 106, 107; David Muench: p. 113; Claus Mroczynski: p. 112; Steve Mulligan: p. 111; National Archives: p. 32, 54 (drawing), 66 (letters); John Ninnemann: p. 69; Laurence Parent: p. 20, 110; San Juan Productions: p. 50 (accident), 68 (top center), 101 (main photo); University of Arizona Library: p. 8 (diary); University of Nebraska, Archives and Special Collections: p. 99; University of Utah: p. 7, 8 (map); D. J. Webb: p. 98; William and Merrie Winkler: p. 61 (color photo and menu).

INDEX

**Page numbers in bold print
refer to photos and paintings**